Video Poker Strategy

YOU HAVE	DRAW
4 OF A ROYAL	1
3 OF A KIND	2
4 OF ST FLUSH	1
3 OF A ROYAL	2
2 PAIR	1
HIGH PAIR	3
4 OF A FLUSH	1
RAIGHT	1
ROYAL	3
R	3
GHT	1
USH	2
D	4

ens, kings, aces; STRAIGHTS: Open
LO┤ ve cards excluding
end, an inside card.
an ac down until you find
Start your ha traights or better.
This st...y is royal-biased; the royal flush
is crucial to your chances for success.

D1360379

Roulette Strategy

Clocking The Dealer

The essence of clocking a dealer is to
determine if there is any pattern to the
number on the wheel where the ball is
released, and the section of the wheel where
the ball lands. Experienced roulette dealers
tend to spin the ball and the wheel at
remarkably consistent speeds.
See book text for more details.

Blackjack Basic Strategy

	DEALER UP-CARD									
	2	3	4	5	6	7	8	9	10	A
8	H	H	H	H	H	H	H	H	H	H
9	H	D	D	D	D	H	H	H	H	H
10	D	D	D	D	D	D	D	D	H	H
11	D	D	D	D	D	D	D	D	D	H
12	H	H	S	S	S	H	H	H	H	H
13	S	S	S	S	S	H	H	H	H	H
14	S	S	S	S	S	H	H	H	H	H
15	S	S	S	S	S	H	H	H	H	H
16	S	S	S	S	S	H	H	H	H	H
A-2	H	H	H	D	D	H	H	H	H	H
A-3	H	H	H	D	D	H	H	H	H	H
A-4	H	H	D	D	D	H	H	H	H	H
A-5	H	H	D	D	D	H	H	H	H	H
A-6	H	D	D	D	D	H	H	H	H	H
A-7	S	S	S	D	D	S	S	H	H	H
A-8	S	S	S	S	S	S	S	S	S	S
A-9	S	S	S	S	S	S	S	S	S	S
2-2	H	H	SP	SP	SP	SP	H	H	H	H
3-3	H	H	SP	SP	SP	SP	H	H	H	H
4-4	H	H	H	SP	SP	H	H	H	H	H
5-5	D	D	D	D	D	D	D	D	H	H
6-6	SP	SP	SP	SP	SP	H	H	H	H	H
7-7	SP	SP	SP	SP	SP	SP	H	H	H	H
8-8	SP	SP	SP	SP	SP	SP	SP	SP	SP	SP
9-9	SP	SP	SP	SP	SP	S	SP	SP	S	S
10-10	S	S	S	S	S	S	S	S	S	S
A-A	SP	SP	SP	SP	SP	SP	SP	SP	SP	SP

H=HIT   S=STAND   D=DOUBLE   SP=SPLIT

P L A Y E R   H A N D

More Cards Inside Back Cover

Budget Gambling™

Look for this optimum paytable:

ROYAL FLUSH	4000*
ST FLUSH	50
4 OF A KIND	25
FULL HOUSE	**9**
FLUSH	**6**
STRAIGHT	4
3 OF A KIND	3
TWO PAIR	2
JACKS OR BETTER	1

*Bonus for 5 coins (some machines pay a 5000-coin bonus—always look for the maximum payout).

This is a "6-9" machine. A "5-8" machine pays 5 coins for a flush and 8 coins for a full house. Never play if less than a 5-8 machine. Be sure jacks-or-better returns your bet and two pair pays 2 coins. **ALWAYS PLAY 5 COINS.**

© 1999 by John Gollehon

ROULETTE PAYTABLES			DOUBLE ZERO		SINGLE ZERO	
TYPE OF WAGER	NUMBERS COVERED	ACTUAL PAYOFF	CORRECT ODDS	HOUSE EDGE	CORRECT ODDS	HOUSE EDGE
Straight-Up	1	35:1	37:1	5.26	36:1	2.70
Split	2	17:1	18:1	5.26	17.5:1	2.70
Street	3	11:1	11.7:1	5.26	11.3:1	2.70
Corner	4	8:1	8.5:1	5.26	8.25:1	2.70
Five-Number	5	6:1	6.6:1	7.89	Not Available	
Line	6	5:1	5.3:1	5.26	5.17:1	2.70
Column	12	2:1	2.2:1	5.26	2.1:1	2.70
Dozen	12	2:1	2.2:1	5.26	2.1:1	2.70
Red/Black	18	1:1	1.1:1 (1.05:1)	5.26 (2.63)	1.05:1 (1.03:1)	2.70 (1.35)
Odd/Even	18	1:1	1.1:1 (1.05:1)	5.26 (2.63)	1.05:1 (1.03:1)	2.70 (1.35)
1-18/19-36	18	1:1	1.1:1 (1.05:1)	5.26 (2.63)	1.05:1 (1.03:1)	2.70 (1.35)

The numbers in parentheses are the odds and percentages for either "surrender" or "en prison" that some casinos permit on the even-money wagers.

© 1999 by John Gollehon

Budget Gambling™

Every possible player hand and dealer up-card combination is shown on the reverse side. Take this card with you to the tables. Most casinos will let you use it provided you do not slow down the game.

Beginners should sit at the far left so that more time is available to evaluate their hand. The following chart shows you how basic strategy can help you overcome the disadvantage of having to draw first:

DISADVANTAGE

Player must draw first   –7.0 %

ADVANTAGE

Blackjack pays 3 to 2	+2.5
Double when favorable	+1.5
Split when favorable	+0.5
Hit and Stand correctly	+2.5

You should receive an untied blackjack about once every 21 hands. Do not insure a blackjack. If you do not receive a blackjack as often as noted, change tables. Playing correct basic strategy makes blackjack a nearly even game, but does not guarantee that you will win.

© 1999 by John Gollehon

Budget Gambling™

John Gollehon

GOLLEHON BOOKS™
GRAND RAPIDS, MICHIGAN

Library of Congress Catalog Card Number 99-94315

ISBN 0-914839-48-9
(International Standard Book Number)

GOLLEHON and BUDGET GAMBLING are exclusive
trademarks of Gollehon Press, Inc.

GOLLEHON BOOKS are published by: Gollehon Press, Inc.,
6157 28th St. SE, Grand Rapids, MI 49546.

GOLLEHON BOOKS are available in quantity purchases; contact
Special Sales. Gollehon does not accept unsolicited manuscripts. Brief
book proposals are reviewed.

Contents

Other Books Authored By John Gollehon

Casino Games
Casino Games II
Pay The Line
A Gambler's Little Instruction Book
A Gambler's Bedside Reader

The All About Series:
All About Blackjack
All About Craps
All About Slots And Video Poker
All About Roulette
All About Baccarat
All About Sports Betting
All About Keno

From The Author...

The decision to gamble is a personal one. It should take into account many things, not the least of which is your ability to wisely manage money. If you frequently overdraw your checking account, exceed your credit-card limits, or otherwise spend your money recklessly—buying on impulse, for example—suffice to say, gambling is a bad idea.

If you do decide to try your luck, promise yourself that you will stay within your means. Gambling can be fun. Don't let serious losses take your fun away.

Acknowledgments

I would like to thank three of my horse-racing
friends who came to my aid when I was putting
the strategies together for the horse-racing
chapters. I had spent considerable time tweaking
my strategies to reflect today's changes in the
industry. Obviously, it was important to test them
again before publication. I tip my hat to:

Mark Lewis
David Santorine
John Alcamo

Now, about all those big trifectas you guys hit...
how do you propose we split 'em up?

When you play,
play with caution,
play with patience.
You can't win
without them.

—*John Gollehon*

Five Against Four

When new players confront me and ask me what their chances really are of winning, I have a stock answer for them, and I'd like to share it with you.

I tell them it's "five against four." You're the four; the casino's the five.

It's not as bad as when you were a kid and two bullies went after you, two against one. But now those same two bullies own a casino, and they're after you again. But this time the odds are a little better: They've picked up three guys, and you've picked up three. That's five against four. Better, but still not a fair fight.

It's like playing a basketball game against the usual five players, but your team is a player short.

Your team is 20 percent short, which is about what the casino's drop percentages are at all the games. Not the game percentages, mind you, but the overall amount of money most players lose from their bankroll—on average—each session, each visit, each trip. Think of it as a percentage of loss *because* of the game percentages... because you keep churning over your bets, letting that small game-percentage eat away at your bankroll.

The strategies in *Budget Gambling,* are designed to try to minimize the effects of game percentages, but we have to be realistic, too. You should know that my advice and strategies are not offered with the promise in mind of making you rich, or preventing you from losing. If you have any strategies that can do that, you send me *yours*!

My strategies are offered to help you enjoy gambling, while, at the same time, provide an opportunity of improving your chances of winning.

Enjoy the moment!

John Gollehon

To the gods of Chance...
Give us one.

CHAPTER 1

Benefits Of
Budget Gambling

Of all the things that are free in a casino, the one thing that's doled out more than anything else, free for the asking, is... you guessed it... advice.

You'll get it from the slot attendants, experts that they are:

"Play that machine over there. It hasn't hit in a long time."

"Yeah, well, is that good?" asks the player.

"Oh yeah!" says the attendant. "That means it's overdue!"

Pu-leeze! Slot machines are never "overdue." These cold-metal machines couldn't care less if they've paid out or not, and they certainly aren't holding back, just waiting for *you* to sit down... but they do have brains! Today, all slot machines are driven by computer chips that determine the timing of payouts. It's the chip, stupid. But try to tell that to a slot attendant.

Dealers love to give advice, too, especially in the past tense:

"You should have stayed on your 16."

"Hmmm, yeah, I guess you're right," says the player who just watched the dealer scoop up his chips.

Most players just assume that dealers really do know the right moves because, after all, they do this eight hours a day. It's their living. They must be good at it. But good at what? Hey, it's a lot easier to figure out that you should have stood on that crummy 16 *after* you watched the dealer bust. Hindsight is always 20/20. I suppose that explains why you never see dealers wearing glasses.

Your gambling friends and buddies are quick to point our your mistakes, too. It would almost seem as if everyone in the casino, except you, is an expert, ready to dish out advice, even when you don't want it:

"How come you changed from red to black?" says your roulette buddy. "You won three bets in a row on red. Why change now?"

Actually, your buddy's kinda right... and kinda wrong. Truth is, there is no right or wrong advice at the roulette table. Roulette is a guessing game. You either guess right or you guess wrong. If someone gives you advice, it's no better a guess than your own.

And then there are pit bosses. In all my years of casino gambling, I can't forget the worst advice

I've ever heard, and it came from someone who should have known better. That's right. A pit boss. Are you ready for this gem?

And the winner is:

"If you want to win thousands of dollars, you have to bet thousands of dollars."

The dubious honor of this award goes to a cocky pit boss standing behind a blackjack table in Reno, Nevada. Yep. You can probably paint the scene yourself. A player stands up, pushes away his chair, gathers in his seventy-five bucks in winnings, and says to the pit boss, "I'm a good player, but I'm never going to get rich at this game."

It's hard to figure why someone would complain about winning. I can understand complaining about losing, but this guy walked away with more chips than he started with. It's almost as if he deserved the world's worst gambling advice: "Look buddy, if you want to win thousands of dollars, you have to bet thousands of dollars."

Well, this smart-aleck pit boss never met ol' Gus, a retired autoworker from Detroit. Gus tagged along with some friends on a trip to Las Vegas. It would be his first go at casino gambling, so he smartly read up on blackjack, a game that he had heard could be beaten with skill.

Skill, shmill. Little did Gus know that he would make gambling history with a run of luck that remains unchallenged even to this day.

Gus chose the first table he saw that had the fewest players. After all, if he was to embarrass himself, he didn't want to do it at a crowded table. He settles in, fidgets a little, and then stretches to one side so he can fish out some money from his pocket. He finds a wadded-up five-dollar bill and neatly places it beyond the betting circle. The dealer rolls her eyes as she tries to straighten out the bill.

"Give me five silver dollars," he says, with that rookie smile that every poker player loves to see. The way that bill looked, all faded and torn, he was lucky if someone would give him four-fifty for it.

"We don't have silver dollars, sir. We use one-dollar chips."

"Oh, OK, give me five chips then."

Gus counts the five chips, stores four, and places one chip in the betting circle.

"This is a five-dollar game, sir," says the dealer with another roll of her eyes.

"You mean I have to bet it all?"

"Yeah, that's right. The whole shebang."

Fortunately for Gus, he won that bet, and the next, and the next. And not being an experienced player, he wasn't sure if what was happening was all that unusual. He was dealt so many pat hands that there really wasn't much thinking to do. "I'm good," he would say, cuing the dealer to roll her eyes and remind him for the umpteenth time, "I need a hand signal, sir," but Gus would just keep saying, "I'm good." And the dealer would resign herself to saying, "I know."

Allow me to cut to the ninth inning. The book Gus read preached the importance of incremental betting... increasing the amount of your wager each time you win. And what a time to do it.

Gus won 38 out of 40 hands! Halfway through the shoe, Gus had worked his way up to black chips; his incredible run had summoned two pit bosses to his table. But there was no counting going on. Gus hadn't read that far. The bosses decided there was no point in a new shuffle; Gus was simply getting good hands. One right after another. And on those rare times he didn't, the dealer would kindly bust. It wasn't hard to figure out just exactly how this rookie of all rookies was making such a killing.

He was just plain lucky.

But he was also smart. Had Gus stuck to his five-dollar bets, he would have won a tidy sum of $180. But Gus knew better. He increased his bets as he continued to win and ended up with over ten thousand dollars! It had nothing to do with his skill of the game, but with his skill in betting.

What is significant here is that Gus never put himself in jeopardy. He did not start out by risking "thousands of dollars." He did not risk any appreciable sum. He came to the table with a five-dollar bill. A toothpick. And he walked away with a lumberyard.

Budget Gambling at its best!

Three Different Strategies To Choose From

The story you just read is important not only because it shows you an example of *Budget Gambling's* potential for success, but also because it lays bare the old way of thinking as to how to produce big wins. ***Budget Gambling*** is new ad-

vice. **It's a new idea. It's the new way to play.**
And it's so much more than what you're probably
thinking it is. Let me tell you more about it right
now so that you are clear on this exciting new concept before we get too far along.

You see, *Budget Gambling* **is comprised of**
three different strategies of betting, all based on
a "low risk, high reward" concept. You've just
witnessed the most basic of the three, called *Pro-*
gressive Betting. It applies to games, mostly table
games, where the payoffs are at even money.

For those bets that pay more than even money—
certain roulette and craps bets, for example—your
betting strategy is called *Proposition Betting*. It's
easy to learn and offers the lowest risk-to-reward
ratio. The third strategy, perhaps the most exciting
of all, is called *Parlay Betting*. You can use this
strategy at most games, although its roots come
from betting methods more commonly found in
horse racing and sports betting. A version of parlay betting I designed for blackjack, called Double
Double, has helped me reap big wins in relatively
short sessions. It's easy, and fully explained in the
chapter on blackjack.

Who Can Benefit
From *Budget Gambling?*

So, is *Budget Gambling* for everyone? Darn
near. Or, at least, it should be. The only players
we can easily exclude from *Budget Gambling* are
high rollers. You know, the players who *do* begin
with big bets. Such players, who like our pit-boss
friend was alluding to, think that the only way they

can win big is to bet big, right out of the chute! This dangerous notion is entirely hogwash. **You *can* win big without betting big! That's the whole idea of *Budget Gambling!***

The only assurance I can give players who start out with big bets is this: Big losses! Maybe not *every* time but *some* time. And for players like you and me, why take that risk? Indeed. The players who *will* take that risk have money trees growing in their back yard. But having big money is certainly no reason to bet big money. If you are so fortunate to have a lot of money, and you intend to get your thrills and spills by risking it, you're barking up the wrong tree! You're reading the wrong book!

The other possible exception to players who are right for *Budget Gambling* are those whom I call "by the book" players. They make only the low-percentage bets, trying to grind out a few dollars through the most tedious, disciplined play imaginable. I don't fault this type of gambler at all. In fact, it's the way I played for many years. But as you're about to learn, this is not the description of the typical player today. It's not what most players are looking for. Sure, most players want the low risk of low-percentage bets, but they also want high rewards. They want *both*. And in *Budget Gambling*, I'm going to try to give it to them.

The Four Important Traits
Of *Budget Gambling*

As a result of my many years studying the games and, particularly, the players, it became clear to me what most players really want from gambling. Obviously, players want to win, but it's *how* they win that determined the four important traits of *Budget Gambling* that make it unique. First and foremost, players want those wins with low risk and high rewards. As any good stockbroker would attest to, it's first on the list of most all new investors. And it's exactly what "investors" in the casino want also: token investments; big returns.

Most all players—even if they don't want to admit it—not only want to win big with little risk, but they also want to win both easily and quickly. It's a sign of the times, I suppose. And it's a tall order. It's why there are fewer players at the racetrack today and more players in casinos. The decisions are faster in the casino—some would say, too fast—and the work factor associated with handicapping is nearly non-existent in the casino.

My analysis also explains why most patrons in casinos today are slot players. Slots definitely offer low risk and high rewards. Just ask the player who won five thousand dollars playing a nickel slot! And slot machines are certainly fast. As fast as you can load 'em up, push the buttons or pull the handle. With the exception of certain skill machines such as video poker, there is absolutely nothing to learn, nothing to study, nothing to memorize. Who would argue that slots are easy to play?

All of this also explains why blackjack has become somewhat flat over recent years. New players coming up soon realize that they must really bone up on the game to have any chance at winning. Only a few make that decision to "work" at the game, to really learn it, much as a chess player must do to really appreciate the complexity and strategy of the game.

Too many players also pass up the craps tables for much the same reason. The table layout looks complicated, even though the game is gosh-awful easy to play.

Keno is also getting less and less play, but not because the game is difficult to learn (it isn't) but because it is too darn slow. In some casinos, games are played every 15 minutes. And what do players do between games? Nothing, I suppose, except wait for the next one. One might as well wait in a doctor's office. Waiting is waiting, right? But no one likes to wait. Waiting is not fun.

And that's the fourth attribute of my betting strategies. It's what losing isn't. It's what work isn't. It's what waiting isn't. That's right. *Gambling has to be fun*. Otherwise, we wouldn't do it, would we? Above all, players need to enjoy the fun of gambling. And don't tell me that fun is automatic with winning. Winning isn't always fun. Just ask the dice player who had to fight tooth and nail to come back with a token win after being down thousands of dollars. That *isn't* fun. Take my word for it.

My strategies will help you enjoy gambling even when you don't win. I can't ensure that you'll win every time, or even more times than not. No one can do that for you. But by keeping your losses in check, you'll be able to enjoy what I believe is the real essence of gambling: the *anticipation* of winning. And the bigger the better! It's what drives us all to try our luck. All we want is a chance to beat the odds.

So there you have it. *Budget Gambling* is based on what most all players really want out of gambling: (1) a low-risk, high-reward ratio, (2) an enjoyable pace, (3) ease of play, and (4) a fun experience.

Is there a trade-off to all this, you ask? Oh, sure. In order to combine low risk with high reward, you will often find yourself making bets that are not the lowest percentage available. But that's the price you pay. Most games are designed with higher percentages hidden in the higher payoffs. It makes sense from a design point of view, doesn't it? If you're a game designer, and you want to take a big chunk out of a player's win for the house, take it out of a bigger win instead of a smaller one. The designer's theory is that players will be so happy with the big wins that they won't realize, much less think about, the "juice" the casino just stuck in its back pocket. But we can deal with this, as you'll see as we go along.

Another factor that comes into play with proposition betting is the odds you're bucking in going after the higher-payout bets. But the thrill of hitting a big multiple-odds payoff, such as 9 to 1 at the dice tables, is pure gambling fun.

Parlay betting is based on winning multiple bets much like progressive betting, but the bets can be either multiple-odds or even-money payoffs. Parlay betting requires a specific string of even-money wins (usually three), or a short progression of higher-odds wagers, designed so that you can win immediately while building your potential exponentially. As you can imagine, parlay betting poses a much greater challenge but with far greater rewards. Nothing can beat the sheer jubilance of watching your second press win at the blackjack tables as you turn $10 into $80!

Budget Gambling Compared To Optimum Betting

Each set of chapters that follows is for a particular game. I'll describe the game for you so you'll understand it, but I won't overwhelm you with technical and mathematical details that you probably don't care about, anyhow. Most important, I'll tell you the different ways you can play the games using as many of the *Budget Gambling* strategies as possible. But I'll also show you the optimum way to play. You might decide, however, as many other players have, that *Optimum Betting* does not always give you everything you want from gambling. Still, it will be there for you, at least for comparison.

I know you're wondering exactly what optimum betting is, so let me give you a précis right now before we continue. Optimum betting at the blackjack tables, for example, means that you only bet more when the cards are running in your favor. You see, blackjack is a game of continually changing percentages. You must keep track of the cards played and adjust your bets based on this varying percentage. But how do you know what the percentage is at any particular time? The percentage will expose itself through "card-counting." It isn't easy. And for most players, it takes the fun out of the game. But it is certainly the optimum way to play. *Bet more when the percentage is in your favor; bet less, or not at all, when the percentage is running against you.*

Optimum betting has nothing to do with progressions or any other systematic form of betting. If it were not for casino countermeasures installed to thwart card-counters, I would recommend this method exclusively over all others. Only those of you who have experienced the frustrations of card-counting can appreciate what I'm saying. Put another way, card-counting strategies work great in theory, but the game isn't played on paper; it's played in the real world, in casinos that let go of their money very, very hard.

When we get to the chapter on blackjack strategies, *I'll show you a way to count cards that does not really involve memorizing. Card-counting is too important to simply dismiss as too frustrating to practice.* The trick, as you'll see, is to make it less of a chore and more of a fun thing to do, in the true tradition of *Budget Gambling*.

At the dice tables, optimum betting means pass-line and come wagers with full odds. And that's it. All other bets (and there are lots of them!) present too high a percentage to be considered an optimum bet. And you thought card-counting took the fun out of blackjack? Try standing around a dice table, making only these basic bets. Even though it's the optimum way to play, it certainly is not the most exciting. Once again, however, *Budget Gambling* comes to the rescue, as you'll learn in our chapter on craps strategies.

At the racetrack, optimum betting is based on a careful study of a racing form or program, in the hope of picking a winning horse, even if it means earning a paltry $2.20 for every $2 you wager. Not too exciting, is it? But it's the optimum way to stay in the game.

You should know that optimum betting only benefits the long-term player. Nothing says that higher-percentage bets won't win more (or lose less) in the short term. And, as you'll learn later, playing in the short term is indeed smarter than long-term exposure.

Optimum betting requires extreme discipline, particularly at the blackjack tables. You are, after all, eating the low-cal stuff that's good for you, and taking a pass on the strawberry cheesecake. I mean, what good is salad without all that stuff to put on it? And who wants mashed potatoes without gravy? A baked potato without sour cream and butter? I'll save you a lot of time studying up on these games. The fun bets are not always the good bets. The fun bets might have all the calories.

What's nice about *Budget Gambling* is that you can partake of some of these delicious bets without putting your health in jeopardy. Since most of these bets are low-risk (small wagers), with high odds (large payoffs), they do provide an opportunity for big wins without the accompanying risk of large initial wagers. Horse racing is a good example. With *Budget Gambling,* there's no need to study a form or program; you simply let the changing odds determine your picks. And you can bet the more exciting long-odds bets like trifectas, where a $2 ticket might earn you hundreds of times your wager!

A Personalized Strategy Designed Just For You

So now you know what *Budget Gambling* is.

Among your choices of strategies, **proposition betting requires only modest bets. You're relying on the higher-odds payoffs to reap big wins.** Players like it because they're never required to make large wagers, even if they have substantial wins in their pockets. Why is this offered? Because some players just don't want to make the bigger progressive bets, period. Even if they are winning bet after bet, the idea of betting big just doesn't suit them. Years ago, I recognized this trait of many players. It's the reason I designed proposition betting. For you players with timid betting habits, proposition betting gives you the opportunity of hitting some big payoffs in spite of your self-imposed betting restrictions.

For those of you who don't mind betting some of your winnings right back at the casino, **progressive betting requires only modest bets at the outset, but calls for some bigger bets as you progress up a winning streak. It is a simple, yet effective, strategy of reinvesting a portion of your winnings.**

Some casino games simply are not designed for all three types of strategies, but in most all cases, I can provide at least a variation or two, or what amounts to a combination of both the progressive and proposition strategies. **Parlay betting offers you the benefits of both of the other strategies, while providing perhaps the most favorable risk-to-reward potential.** In some cases, you'll parlay your winnings with your wager and slam-dunk the casino. In other cases, a portion of your winnings will press in the hope of winning a short sequence of multiple-odds payoffs. Parlay betting might be the betting choice for many players, but look them all over before you begin, to see which strategy is best suited for you.

Modest initial betting is the defining attribute of all the *Budget Gambling* strategies. It's a common thread in all the betting strategies you encounter here. Your initial bets may stay modest, or increase, as your play continues depending on your success and the strategy you choose.

Think of my strategies as being personalized just for you. In a sense, they are. The strategies, as I said earlier, are based on the playing habits of literally thousands of players I've witnessed over the years.

Regardless of the strategy you choose, please understand that you must be comfortable with your betting. If, at any time, you're not comfortable with what you're doing, don't do it. Gambling, with all of it's inherent stress, can become insurmountable if you are the least bit uncomfortable with your play. You must have confidence in what you're doing, tempered with patience and caution.

These three important betting disciplines: confidence, patience, and caution, are the hallmark of successful players.

15

CHAPTER 2

The Most Powerful Strategy

You'll have fun reading about all the *Budget Gambling* strategies I'm going to give you, and then actually testing the ones that sound good to you. The strategies will add an entirely new dimension to your play.

As you recall, the strategies are all based on either progressive, proposition, or parlay betting. Among these, the Four-Color Progressive Strategy is far and away the most powerful to use. My critics rate it as one of the most intriguing progressions I've ever designed.

This special strategy can be used for all three of the major table-games: craps, blackjack, and roulette. Expect a variation here or there for each game. Because of its frequent use, I believe it would be more helpful to you if we detail the Four Color right here in its own chapter, before we even start talking about the rules of the games. Once you learn the basics of this strategy, the chapters on game-betting will be a breeze for you.

Now that we're ready to talk about a particular strategy in detail, it's important that you understand another basic set of tenets on which my strategies are based:

All *Budget Gambling* strategies are based on the concept that in any negative-expectation game, the keys to success are in (1) minimizing the number of decisions, (2) maximizing the wins in winning decisions, and (3) minimizing the losses in losing decisions.

By letting patience and frequent exits play a big role in our betting strategies—not to mention the very nature of the bets we will be making, such as avoiding the one-roll bets at craps—we have already taken a good turn at key #1. All that's left to do is unleash our winning potential, while holding losses to a minimum.

Evolution Of The Four-Color Progressive Strategy

The Four-Color Progressive Strategy combines the advantages of optimum betting (making only the lowest percentage bets) with a mathematically proven betting progression. It *will* help you maximize winnings and minimize losses.

The Four Color even has built-in rules to help minimize exposure. Whether it keeps you out of the long term, however, is up to you. Only you can decide exactly how attached you want to become to your friendly, neighborhood casino.

Allow me to provide you with a little history. The Four Color is based on my original Gollehon Betting Strategy, which was first published in *Casino Games II* many years ago. The strategy was tied to the mathematical frequencies of streaks—larger increases at the beginning, tailoring to smaller increases as a streak continues. In creating the Four Color, I redesigned these incremental steps to provide the same benefit *within each level,* so that players unable to make it far into the progression could still gain this advantage entirely within the first level... the easiest to reach.

The original Gollehon Betting Strategy proved to be ideal for blackjack and roulette, but not for craps because of the odd betting increments that my computer formula required. Some bets might be $13, some $28... like I said, OK at a blackjack table, and certainly at a roulette table, but difficult at a dice table where bets are routinely made in chip-value multiples ($5, $10, $15 and so on) or odds payoff multiples, as in the case of place-bets on the 6 and 8 ($6, $12, $18, and so on).

Although it's perfectly fine to make a $13 bet on the pass-line, and back it up with $26 in odds, you'll get some funny looks from the dealers, and both you and the dealer will have to do some quick figuring to determine the payoffs. Truth is, the idea of making bets in chip-value multiples, primarily multiples of $5, is a logical one, and it certainly makes the game easier to play. So I relinquished.

Years later, I devised a special progressive strategy for craps that I called Power Betting, It was introduced in the publication of *Conquering Casino Craps,* and it's still going strong. In fact, most of the queries my office receives relates in some way to Power Betting. It's all the proof I need that craps continues to grow in popularity. In fact, more so than blackjack. But it also tells me that players appreciate a good strategy to help organize their betting and keep it in check.

More important, a good betting strategy fulfills a purpose; call it *reason*. There's reason to your methods. There is no reason to haphazard betting. You'll understand this better if you think of my strategies as a pathway to your goals.

The Four-Color Progressive Strategy has become a hybrid of both the Gollehon Betting Strategy and Power Betting. Where the GBS is best for blackjack and roulette, and Power Betting is only for craps, the Four Color is perfect for *all* casino games, including craps. Especially craps! Plus, it is easier to use with fewer rules to remember. And, it is more conservative at the beginning, which is important for most players, including you, I would imagine, because that's why you picked up this book, right? Indeed. **We want to minimize risk, so we establish safe, minimum betting habits at the outset.**

As I present The Four-Color Progressive Strategy to you, I'm reminded of what we talked about in the first chapter... that too many players today want "easy" and they want "quick." I can make the strategies easy, and, to some extent, quick, but

I want you to know right now that "quick" can be a detriment to winning. Players who want to win quickly are the same people who tend to bet recklessly.

I'm not going to compromise my strategies just because some players are so wound up with gambling that they need rapid-fire decisions. I want you to learn how to replace your desire for speed with an enjoyment of "anticipation."

You'll learn that of all the places where patience is a virtue, none is a better example than the casino. I honestly don't believe players can win with even a modicum of consistency if they do not display patience.

The Four-Color Progressive Strategy

	5	
	5	PRE-PLAY
	5	
	10	
	15	RED LEVEL
	20	
Repeat Option	**25**	
	50	GREEN LEVEL
	75	
Repeat Option	**100**	
	200	BLACK LEVEL
	300	
Repeat Option	**400**	
	800	
	1200	PURPLE LEVEL
	1600	
	2000	

Four-Color Progressive Strategy Advantages

- Makes your betting virtually automatic. There are no tough decisions to make. Nothing to ponder. You simply let the strategy do the work!
- Gives you "out of the gate" protection against sudden losses.
- Ensures a big payday during a hot streak.
- Forces you to bet down or quit during a cold streak.
- Works at all table games.

The Four-Color Progressive Strategy Overview

Before we go over the important rules for this strategy, let's talk a little about how the strategy works. You might think the design looks rather basic, but there's more to it than meets the eye.

Note that there are five levels to the progression, beginning with pre-play. **Pre-play is your safe harbor. You are not allowed to leave pre-play and enter the progression until you have won three bets in a row.** As a further protection, you must quit the session in pre-play if your starting stake of $40 is every reduced to $20. You will always leave the table with no less than $20.

Once you enter the progression, continue to increase your bet to the next amount listed as you continue to win. **If you lose at any time during the run, your next bet, called a "drop-down" bet, will always be three betting amounts lower. If you lose that bet, too, it's time to exit the session.**

21

Remember it this way: **It takes three wins to get in, two losses to get out.**

Chip Color Matches Betting Level

LEVEL	CHIP VALUE
Pre-play/Red	Red $5 Chips
Green	Green $25 Chips
Black	Black $100 Chips
Purple	Purple $500 Chips

Each level will be easy to identify as you play, because your bets will be in the chip color of the levels. Now you know where the name of the strategy came from.

In the first level, you'll play with red ($5) chips, just as you will in pre-play. But in the green level, you'll progress to green ($25) chips. In the black level (everyone's favorite), you'll be betting black ($100) chips... and holding onto your seat. Because the next level, if you get to it, is where the mega-money is: The purple level means you'll be betting purple ($500) chips. Technically, the second bet of this level goes to purple, but it's close enough. (Some casinos use a different color for their $500 chips, but who cares what color they are as long as there are two nice round zeros after the 5.)

Incidentally, if you need to change color as you proceed up the progression, by all means do this. Simply ask the dealer to change your stack of 20 red chips to four green chips, for example. Some dealers tend to pay off bets in the same color, but you want to get "new" color in your payoffs so you can have the right color to start the next level.

It's important that you use the chip colors correctly as you go up the progression. **Using the right chip colors minimizes the number of chips in a bet, makes payoffs easier, and helps you to know exactly where you are in the progression.**

An interesting design element of this new progression can be noted with each "transition" bet, the first bet of a new level. Note that this wager is only one unit higher than the previous level, and, in a sense, follows the previous level's progression. This transition bet was carefully designed into the strategy to help ease you along to the next level while extending the diminishing percentage of increase within a four-bet run (10, 15, 20, 25, for example).

The Four-Color Strategy's Transition Bets

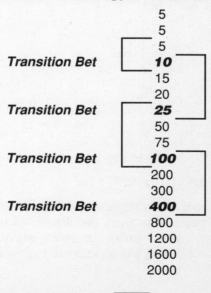

```
                          5
                          5
                          5
Transition Bet           10
                          15
                          20
Transition Bet           25
                          50
                          75
Transition Bet          100
                         200
                         300
Transition Bet          400
                         800
                        1200
                        1600
                        2000
```

The Four-Color Progressive Strategy Rules

IMPORTANT: The progression, per se, is only a part of the strategy, which will not work for you if the strategy rules are not adhered to. *Following the rules is just as important as following the progression.*

1. Take to the session a stake of $40.
2. Enter the session with a pre-play bet of $5.
3. Exit the session if (a) you lose two bets in a row, or (b) your stake drops to $20.
4. Enter the progression only after you win three bets in a row.
5. Increase your bet to the next betting amount shown in the progression as long as you continue to win each bet.
6. Decrease your bet by three betting amounts following a loss in the progression. This bet is called a "drop-down" bet.
7. If the drop-down bet wins, continue the progression from that point. If the drop-down bet loses, you must exit the session subject to rule 3a.
8. If you make multiple bets, each bet is treated independently.

Explanation Of The Rules

Rule 1: Learn how to start each session with the same-size stake. All good gamblers I know do this. It's a mark of discipline. Don't walk up to a table and fish around in your pockets for whatever you can scrounge up. Do you think this looks pro? Have two twenties ($40) ready to go. Exchange them for chips by setting the bills on the table directly in front of you (but not within a betting area) while saying, loud and clear: "Change forty dollars, all red chips, please."

Personally, when I do this at a dice table where the whole table is a betting area, I purposely lay the bills across part of the "field" and part of the "come," two adjacent betting areas within easy reach of the dealer. That way, in case I'm confronted with a deaf dealer, there's no question that my money *doesn't* play.

Ultra-conservative players might be concerned about starting out with $40. They shouldn't be. Forty dollars is *not* a loss-limit. On the contrary. Rule 3b limits your loss for the session to $20.

So, why not start out with $20 instead of $40? Because I also want you to learn how to leave a cold table with a goodly portion of your stake. It may only be psychological, since either way it's a $20 smack in the teeth, but I never want to put you in a position where you walk away with nothing. There's no worse feeling.

Incidentally, just because Rule 3a says you walk at $20, that doesn't mean you can't walk earlier. That's something else I don't want to do; I never want to come across as forcing you to play to a certain limit, or for a certain length of time. *Quit whenever you want to*.

The next thing you do after exiting a session is to go to the cage and exchange the remaining chips for cash. And, if you're like me, you'll record the session in your journal. Doing these things has a secondary purpose: It gives you something to do during your break from the tables. You might even want to get a cup of coffee and plan your next session. Whatever you decide to do, *let patience guide you*. I don't want to see you feeling a rush to get back to the tables.

This is an important discipline to follow, so allow me to repeat it: Always cash in your chips when you exit a session. Never begin a session with chips. Always begin a session the same way each time: with cash—two twenties.

If you have won a considerable amount of money from prior sessions, lock up your money, literally. Most casinos offer safety deposit boxes at no charge to you. **Never carry large amounts of cash on your person.**

Another advantage of using a safety deposit box is to keep you away from your winnings. I hate to see players risking more than just a small portion of their winnings for stake money.

Key question: So when do you go back and tackle the table again? Is five minutes too soon? You're darn right it is! Take a break. Relax. Eat lunch. Go for a walk. Check out some other tables. Check out the pool. Check out the action. At the tables, that is. What's the point of quitting a bad table if you're going to head right back?

Rule 2: Pre-play starts with $5. And you'll stay at that betting level until you can string three wins together. Since this strategy will be used only for bets with even-money payoffs, which usually have "decent" percentages, you'll encounter that typical win-one, lose-one scenario often. There is little movement in terms of wins or losses, so the $5 betting limit is not going to be much of an issue. No one would say, "Gee, I wish I were betting $25 instead." Breaking even is breaking even.

If you find yourself winning only one bet out of three—and not that unusual, either—you will be thankful that you are restricted to your $5 limit. If, on the other hand, the table conditions look promising, and you've managed to win three out of three, what better indicator to start moving up a little?

When I mention pre-play to some of my friends who bet much more heavily than I do, I get quite a laugh. "Five bucks? You've got to be kidding!" Funny, isn't it? You don't even have to be a high roller to look down your nose at a five-dollar bill. For the high rollers of the world, $5 isn't even good enough for tip money. And it certainly won't get them any comps, either. Too bad. **This book is for players who want to win money, not comps. It's for players who bet to win, not to impress.**

Let's get serious for a moment. Remember that this rule is for openers. What I call "early betting." Judging the potential of the strategy by the $5 pre-play bet is like watching a quarterback on the opening drive, and then deciding whether or not he's going to carry his team to victory. There's so much of the game left to play! It's how the game ends up, hours later, that counts. Sure, you might have seen him fumble on that opening drive, but now he's piling up the points!

And it's the same thing at the tables. You might start out slowly, but later on you might creep up the progression and run into some decent-sized bets. You might even reach the high roller's level. Trouble is, with these guys, most of them like to *start* with the big bets. And guess what usually happens.

If players were to see me playing at the beginning of a session, they might be surprised—if not bored—watching me bet a thin nickel at the dice table with an even thinner dime for odds. Five dollars on the pass-line and ten bucks in odds is not going to pop many eyes. No jaws are going to drop.

But I'm not bored. And I really don't care what anyone else thinks about the way I play. I know what I'm doing. I'm busy. I'm hunting. Like most players, I'm after the hot shoot that can send me up the progression. Unlike most players, however, I bide my time in getting there, if I get there. Either way, I enjoy the hunt.

Now if those same players were to see me again at that same table a half-hour or so later, it's possible I might be throwing black chips around like candy. I might have a couple of thousand in chips spread over the table with piles more in front of me! Those players might actually confuse me with a high roller. What an insult! But that's what the Four-Color Strategy can do for you!

Rule 3: This important rule protects you against the possibility of getting beaten by a negative streak. By limiting the streak to two, we've nipped it in the bud. We're looking for hot streaks, not cold streaks, so it's time to search elsewhere. Why take the chance that these cold streaks will only continue?

Understand that the lose-two-in-a-row-and-your-out rule applies at any time... in pre-play, or while riding the progression, as Rule 7 also makes clear.

Always keep an eye on your stake. Don't ignore the importance of rule 3b. If your stake ever drops to $20, it's quitting time. It might mean a short session, but who cares. You escaped. You've salvaged half your stake to start a new one. There's always a new session to look forward to. Isn't that right?

Don't think of rule 3b as too strict. It isn't. The critical exit rule is simply to guard against an indiscernible trend. Dice players call this condition "choppy." What it really means is the game is beating you so slowly that you don't realize it. Stop the trend at $20.

Incidentally, don't be concerned that you're exiting sessions too frequently as you apply rule 3. You will definitely find that there are more times than you imagined when the rules tell you to quit. And what you'll be doing is something you probably never did as often as you should have: restricting your losses! But that's not all. As you can appreciate, the best time to restrict your exposure is when you're losing.

Restrict your losses. Restrict your exposure. Two for the price of one.

Rules 4 & 5: This is the fun part! You won your three nickel bets, you've paid your dues, now you're ready to get strapped in and ride the progression! You'll want to take it as far as it will let you.

As long as you win, proceed to the next betting amount. Just let it happen. Don't be nervous. You'll have plenty of protection from previous wins. There are only three places in the progression where a loss might be... well, let's say... less opportune than others. And those spots are where the bets press, as marked with a notation on the chart that says, "Repeat Option." It means exactly what you think. You have the option of repeating the bet before the press. The theory is that winning the repeat option makes you better prepared to lose the press. Personally, I don't make repeat options any more. But you can. It's entirely up to you.

Incidentally, readers write to me on occasion to tell me how high up the progression they've gone. As you can appreciate, most of the time the progression takes you only into the red level. The thinking for most new players is that making it to the green level is just average. No! Getting to the green level is good! *Darn* good!

Getting to the purple level is a great goal to shoot for, but we must be realistic. Reaching the purple level is on a par with hitting 8 out of 8 on a keno ticket. Well, that's not quite true, but the point should be clear. The purple level is an incredible feat!

Rule 6: Yes. All good things do come to an end, sometime. This rule protects you from doing something stupid like continuing the progression after a loss.

There's an old gambler's maxim that certainly applies here: **Never press a loss.** The term *press* means to double the amount of your previous wager in the hope of both winning the bet and making up for the loss.

Indeed, the right move is to *reduce* your bet with a drop-down wager, and that's what Rule 6 tells you to do: Your next bet following a loss in the progression is reduced in proportion to the size of your losing wager. Simply "drop down" three betting amounts and that's your new starting point. Of course, if you were in the red level, your drop-down bet will be in pre-play. And that means you need to follow pre-play rules and win three out of three before you can get out again.

Some players elect to exit the session after a losing bet that ended a lengthy progression. Let's say they were at $100 when they lost the bet. They can't bring themselves to cut back, especially all the way down to a "lowly" $25, so they quit. They had the thrill of betting black, not to mention the thrill of a nice win streak, and they figure they'll be able to appreciate the value of that $25 chip after taking a break, and then starting up again with a nickel on the line. And they are oh-so right. Values diminish as you go back down. After all, you've been there. But going up, you're heading where you probably *haven't* been, which means those betting levels are a new, tasty experience.

So, after a lose, you certainly can quit if you like. Quitting is far superior to continuing the progression, but the smarter choice is to follow Rule 6 and simply cut back by three betting amounts.

31

With all the success you've just had, it's possible the loss was just a blip in your immediate future, and you might be headed right back up again.

Rule 7: This interesting rule covers both situations following a drop-down bet.

If you lose the drop-down wager, that means you lost two bets in a row and you just heard the factory whistle. It's quitting time. No options. No whining. You walk. You exit the session. Your first losing bet, incidentally, was your biggest bet. Your second losing bet was probably big, too, relatively speaking. It would be pure stupidity to risk losing another one.

If you win the drop-down bet while in the progression, continue with the progression at the next amount directly higher than the drop-down bet. For example, if your first loss was $100, your drop-down bet will be $25. If you win that bet, your next wager will be $50. If you lose the $50 bet, your drop-down wager will be $15.

Losses take you down; wins take you up. That's the gist of the Four-Color Strategy. Doesn't it make sense? It should. It should make all the sense in the world to you.

There's something else you should know before we go on to the last rule. We talked about it while discussing Rule 6; we'll talk about it again. There's nothing that says you can't quit instead of returning to pre-play or making a drop-down bet. If you want to quit, quit! In fact, quit any time you want to, although I can't understand why anyone would want to quit while riding a nice win streak. Most often, if players elect to quit on their own (not being forced to quit by rule), it's usually at that moment when they otherwise would have been relegated to pre-play.

But if you do feel like playing some more, follow the pre-play rules and see if you can re-enter the progression. If pre-play doesn't work out and you're forced to exit the session, go outside and get some fresh air. It's probably time for a break, anyhow.

Rule 8: If you decide to make multiple bets, common at the roulette and dice tables, you must learn how to keep track of these bets as they relate to all the rules, because each bet is a separate bet, independent of each other, and subject to all the rules we've just gone over. It isn't hard to do; you just have to maintain the discipline to do it.

It's not unlikely that you might have one bet riding a progression, while another bet or two are resting in pre-play. When you're in the progression, it's easy to tell where you are by simply looking at the size of your wager. *But in pre-play, you need to remember where you stand with the three-out-of-three rule*. Keeping track of one bet is easy. Keeping track of two bets is easy, too. But three bets might take a little doing. Some players I know use a scratch pad. Others keep track by stacking chips in front of them. However you do it, don't release a bet into the progression until it has earned its way.

Minimum Betting

The Four Color Strategy, and most all of the other betting strategies you'll encounter in *Budget Gambling,* are based on a table-minimum wager of $5. But what if you can't find a $5 table? What if you're reading this book many years after I penned it, and the effects of inflation have taken their toll? We all know about inflation, right? In the casino, it means the table minimums go up but the valet who parks your car still gets the same dollar tip.

But even if you're reading *Budget Gambling* in its first printing, you still might have trouble finding a $5 table, especially on holidays and weekends. On Friday night the tables are all $10 minimum. On Monday, and all the other weekdays, those same tables are $5. Well, it's too easy for me to say, "Don't play on holidays or weekends." Some players have no other choice.

You might also have trouble finding a low table-minimum if you play in a market where there is little or no gaming competition. Some one- or two-casino markets have high table-minimums *every* day! And you thought only players were greedy? Guess again.

I have answers to a lot of your gambling problems but I have no answer for this one. **I deplore the concept of setting high table-minimums. I deplore any tactic where the casino is plainly taking advantage of its huge supply of customers. What's worse, I know that most of you will fall for the casino's ploy... because you want to play.**

These higher table-minimums will have a chilling effect on the way you play. Right off the bat you're being pushed, you're being forced into doing something you don't want to do, and you'll find yourself in a foul mood because of it. I can't think of a worse way to begin gambling.

I urge you to look for casinos with reasonable table-minimums, which, outside of Nevada, probably means trying your darndest to play on a weekday.

It is possible to alter the Four-Color Strategy, and other strategies you'll find in *Budget Gambling,* but it's a compromise I don't like. An example would be to start pre-play at $10 (assuming a $10-minimum table) and simply start the red level at $15.

A key concept of *Budget Gambling,* as you know, is to restrict your initial bets to minimum levels until you start winning. If these initial bets are substantial due to high table-minimums, the casino has just defeated your strategy. Like I said, don't give them the opportunity.

The following chapters are in sets of two for each game: an easy chapter on the rules, followed by an even easier chapter on applying the betting skills you've already learned.

The chapters are in the order of the games that I believe give you the best short-term potential without investing a lot of time for study. I mean, this is supposed to be fun, right? So let's start off with the game that should give you the most fun for your dollar.

CHAPTER 3

Craps:
Rules Of The Game

Oh, what fun this game is!

If you enjoy casino gambling, and you've never played craps before, why not? You're missing out on the most exciting game on the casino floor. A win at the dice tables stirs the emotions like you've never experienced. I can't say that it ranks up there with skydiving or bungee-jumping, but for those of us who prefer our excitement on the ground, there aren't many thrill-rides that can beat a red-hot dice table! So buckle up, and let's get this roller-coaster moving!

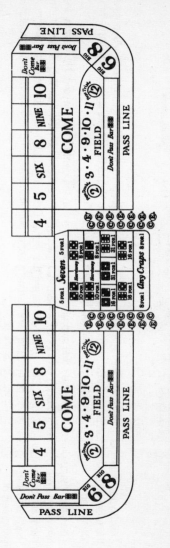

This is a typical Las Vegas layout, although some newer layouts follow the Atlantic City rule of eliminating the "Big 6 and 8" bets on the corners. It's a silly bet that pays 1 to 1 (even money) if a 6 (or 8) is rolled before a 7. The bet should pay 6 to 5. Even a place-bet on 6 or 8 will pay 7 to 6. Players who bet the Big 6 and 8 are showing their inexperience.

Another variation is the field-bet, where some layouts pay double on *both* the 2 and 12. Others pay triple on *either* the 2 or 12, as shown here (triple on 12). Most new casino venues are using the "Las Vegas" layout.

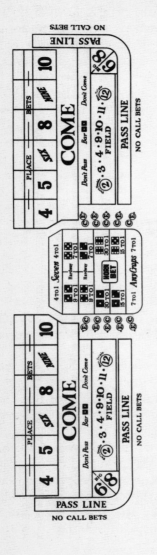

This layout is typical of Northern Nevada casinos. One of the major differences between the two layouts is the location of the "don't pass" and "don't come" sections. The Las Vegas layout has a section reserved for "don't come." Northern Nevada combines the two bets in one section.

The other major difference is the odds expression for "prop bets" in the center of the layout. Notice that the Nevada layout defines the odds payout on a hard 8, for example, as 9 to 1. On the Las Vegas layout, the odds are defined as 10 for 1. Both expressions are the same. Odds of 10 for 1 just sound better and may lead unsuspecting players to believe they are getting a better payoff. It's a cheap ploy the casinos should be ashamed of.

Forget the table layout for a moment. That seems to be what scares away so many new players. Let's pretend that we found a dice table with a spot open, and we're going to walk up and play.

The first thing to notice is that one of the players is the shooter. And that's one of the many neat things about this game. **Craps is the only casino game where the players determine the result of a betting event.** It's as if you and I are allowed to spin the little white ball around the casino's roulette wheel, or deal the cards at the blackjack tables. What fun!

The second thing to notice is that **each end of the table is identical; each end has a dealer responsible for the players and their bets at that particular end of the table.**

We see that the player with the dice is ready to shoot, and off they go, to the opposite end of the table from where the shooter is standing, bouncing off the wall, taking out a player's stack of chips, making a mess but who cares, and finally coming to rest on 7.

We hear a few cheers as we watch the dealers pay all the bets that are positioned between two lines that run all around the perimeter of the table. In between the lines is the word PASS. The 7 was a winning number—it's called "making a pass"— and we've got time now, while the dealers are paying off the bets, to place our own bet on the "pass-line." **Because the pass-line runs all around each end of the table, all the players have a spot right in front of them to make the pass-line bet.** We plunk down a $5 chip and watch as the dealer on *our* side of the table, armed with a stick to retrieve the dice, pushes the two red cubes back to the shooter for another toss.

They blast down the table and land on 11 this time, and more cheers go up because it's another winner for the pass-line. We reach down and pick up our winning $5 chip, leave the original $5 chip on the pass-line, and get ready for another roll of the dice.

This time, the shooter tosses a 6, and there are no more cheers from the players, because a 6 is not a winning number, at least, not just yet. We watch as all the players put more chips down on the table, but they place these chips *behind* the pass-line, directly behind their original pass-line bet, so we do the same. We place two $5 chips behind our single $5 chip on the pass-line.

The shooter is given the dice again, and off they go, landing on 10. There's a lot of hubbub going on as other players are tossing around different bets; in some cases we see the dealers repositioning these bets in numbered boxes, and it looks confusing, but we're not going to pay attention to those bets for now. What's important for us to note is that our money on the pass-line, and all the other players' money on this line, is still there, because the bet is still in doubt. (The shooter is going to keep shooting until either of two numbers is rolled: a 6, in which case the pass-line wins; or a 7, in which case the pass-line loses.)

We watch intensely as the shooter fires the dice again, and before we can even see what happened, we hear cheers going up as we look around to try to find the numbers on the dice. Oh, there they are... one die is hiding behind stacks of chips in front of the dealer, but we can see them now, a 4 and a 2. The shooter made another pass! The pass-line wins!

What's interesting though, as we watch the dealers paying the bets on the pass-line, is that the bet behind the pass-line gets a bonus payoff. We look down at our own bet and see that the dealer gave us $12 in winnings *behind* the line, and $5 in winnings *on* the line. Not bad! What a pleasant surprise!

Let's stop the game for a moment and talk about what we just witnessed. For one thing, we learned that **the number 7 can be a winning number or a losing number.** If the shooter *isn't* trying to repeat a number, then a 7 is indeed a winner. But, if the shooter *is* trying to repeat a number, then a 7 loses. In fact, not only does the pass-line lose, but the shooter also loses the privilege of shooting, and the dice are passed on to the next player who becomes the new shooter (if that player wants to).

If, indeed, that happens, then the next roll of the dice is called a "come-out" roll. **When the dice are coming out, the 7 wins. The 11 wins. But a 2, 3 or 12 loses.** Of all the numbers that can be rolled with a pair of dice: 2, 3, 4, 5, 6, 7, 8, 9, 10, 11, and 12, we now know about five of them.

The remaining six numbers are called "point-numbers," and they must be repeated before a 7 is rolled in order to win. The point-numbers are 4, 5, 6, 8, 9, and 10. Roll a 5 on the come-out, and your task as the shooter is to roll it again. But watch out for that 7, because the 7 will lose.

2–3–12	7–11	4–10	5–9	6–8
Craps (loser)	Natural (winner)	Point-Numbers (must be repeated to win)		

It's important to remember the point-numbers in the pairs as I've listed them. You'll find out why later in this chapter.

The dice are always "coming out" after a pass-line decision. Roll a 7 or 11, and the pass-line wins. The next roll is a come-out roll. Roll a 2, 3, or 12, and the pass-line loses. The next roll is a come-out roll. Roll an 8, and the 8 becomes the shooter's point-number. The next roll is *not* a come-out roll. The next roll, and the next, and the next, and however long it takes to either roll another 8 and win, or roll a 7 and lose, is called "rolling for the point." If the shooter repeats the 8, the pass-line wins and the next roll is a come-out roll. If the shooter rolls a 7, the pass-line loses and the next roll is a come-out roll (with a new shooter). **The shooter only loses the dice after failing to make a point-number (called a "seven-out").** The shooter keeps shooting until a seven-out, even if the shooter throws losers on the pass-line with a 2, 3 or 12, which, incidentally, are called a "craps."

Remember those bets that the players were making behind the pass-line? Well, those bets are called "odds-bets." **Odds-bets are the most important bets you can make at a craps table.** Why? Because the house pays off the odds-bet at the true mathematical odds of actually rolling a point-number before rolling a 7. That's right. The odds-bet is a fair bet; no advantage either way. In fact, *the odds-bet is the only fair bet you can make in the casino*. Always make the odds-bet whenever a shooter is going after a point-number. By doing so, you help to keep the house edge against you as low as possible.

Because the likelihood of rolling point-numbers varies, the payoff varies, too. Here's an easy chart that will help you understand the likelihood of rolling the six different point-numbers before rolling a 7. **Remember these odds because they tell you how much you'll be paid when you win.**

POINT NUMBER	CORRECT ODDS OF REPEATING BEFORE A 7
6 & 8	6 to 5
5 & 9	3 to 2
4 & 10	2 to 1

Most casinos will let you make an odds-bet up to double the amount of your pass-line wager. A few casinos will only allow single odds, an amount equal to your pass-line wager. Still others will allow odds-bets that are triple the amount of your pass-line bet. You might even find a casino offering 10 times odds or more! **Always take the maximum odds unless the bet would become so large that you're not comfortable with the risk.** Generally, double or triple odds is plenty to risk. Don't go overboard on this bet just because you know there's no casino advantage in it. There's always risk. So let common sense guide you along.

What gives craps an overall casino advantage is the seven-out. The players actually have an advantage on the come-out rolls, but the edge quickly swings to the casino when a point-number is established. Here's another chart that shows the frequencies of all the 11 numbers. By now, it can't come as any surprise to you that the 7 is the most likely number to roll. Seasoned dice players know that "the casino owns the 7." In casino parlance, "It's the seven-out that stops the hand."

NUMBER	WAYS	PROBABILITY	HOW
2	1	35 to 1	1-1
3	2	17 to 1	1-2, 2-1
4	3	11 to 1	2-2, 1-3, 3-1
5	4	8 to 1	1-4, 4-1, 2-3, 3-2
6	5	6.2 to 1	3-3, 2-4, 4-2, 1-5, 5-1
7	6	5 to 1	1-6, 6-1, 2-5, 5-2, 3-4, 4-3
8	5	6.2 to 1	4-4, 2-6, 6-2, 3-5, 5-3
9	4	8 to 1	3-6, 6-3, 4-5, 5-4
10	3	11 to 1	5-5, 4-6, 6-4
11	2	17 to 1	5-6, 6-5
12	1	35 to 1	6-6
	36		

Now we know all about the pass-line bet. And isn't it simple? It's not only simple, it's the essence of the game. In fact, you could play the game, and play it well, with all you know at this point. But let's get back to the game to learn more ways we can win!

Now that the dealers have paid the pass-line, the stickperson alerts all the players that the dice are coming out. "Same good shooter," he says, as we quickly bump up our pass-line bet to $10. The dice fly and make the point of 4. Immediately, the dealers place a round "puck" in a box in front of them that's marked "4." **The puck is simply a way of posting the point-number for everyone**

to see. We also note that there are five other boxes in the row, each box represents one of the point-numbers. When you walk up to a dice table, the puck is a quick way for you to find out if the shooter is coming out, or shooting for a point-number. The puck has a black side marked OFF and a white side marked ON. If the dice are coming out, the black side is up. If the shooter is rolling for a point, the puck is placed within the corresponding point-box with the white side up.

We make our odds-bet of $20 and decide to make a new bet in the large box marked COME. We place a $5 chip in the come, positioned so that the chip is directly in front of us. Since other players are making these "come-bets," too, it's important to place the bet directly in front of us, so there's no question the bet belongs to us. What is a come-bet, you ask? **A come-bet is the same as a pass-line wager, except you make it while the shooter is rolling for a point-number. Think of it as a "delayed" pass-line bet.** You can make as many come-bets as you like. And, if the shooter is rolling lots of point-numbers while he tries to repeat his pass-line point-number, a come-bettor will clean up.

The dice are back in the shooter's hands, and we watch intensely as the shooter rolls an 11. We win our come-bet and pick up our $5 in winnings. (Had the shooter rolled a 2, 3, or 12 craps, we would have lost our come-bet. If the shooter rolled a 7, the come-bet would have won, but the pass-line would have lost.)

Here come the dice again, tumbling to the point of 9. The dealers reposition all the come-bets in the point-box marked "9." And how do you suppose they keep track of all these bets? **Come-bets are positioned in relation to the position of the players at the table.** Bets from players standing along the front of the table are positioned along the front side of the point-box. Bets from players standing around the end of the table are positioned along the back side of the point-box.

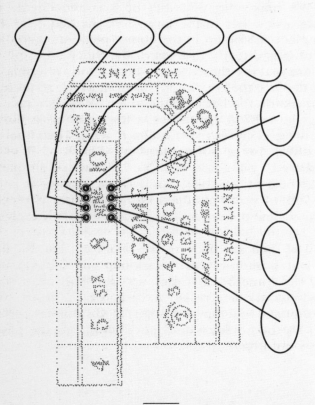

We toss two $5 chips in the come and announce, "Odds on my 9." We watch to make sure the dealer picks up our odds-bet and positions these chips on top of our $5 come-bet slightly off-center to distinguish the odds-bet from our come-bet.

Now we have two numbers working for us: the pass-line point-number 4 and the come-bet point-number 9.

Another roll and what a surprise! The shooter has just repeated the 9! The dealer takes our come-bet and the odds-bet from the point-box of 9 and places these bets back in the come, where they are quickly paid. But all the chips are just left there. It is up to us to pick up these chips before the dice roll again. We count our chips and see that we won $20! We won $5 for our come-bet, and $15 for our odds-bet ($10 paid at 3 to 2 odds).

The shooter is on a roll and everyone's yelling for the 4. The dice bounce hard against the wall of the table and give the players what they've been screaming for: a pair of 2s. "Winner 4, the hard way!" says the stickman, "Pay the line!"

Good thing we bumped up our bet on the pass-line. The point of 4 (and its sister point-number 10) are the hardest to make, so we can expect the highest odds payoff on our odds-bet. We win $10 for our pass-line bet and a whopping $40 for our $20 odds-bet ($10 paid at 2 to 1 odds). How nice of the dealer to give us two green $25 chips! Now we can start "collecting" green! (In most casinos, $1 chips are white or blue, $5 chips are red, $25 chips are green, and $100 chips are black.)

Other Bets

Making pass-line bets and come-bets along with odds-bets (double odds or better) are the smart bets at a dice table because the house edge is as low as you're going to get. With double odds, the house percentage is only six-tenths of a percent! But there are other bets you can make, all with higher percentages.

The next most common bet is called a "place-bet." **Place-bets are made on the same point-numbers as come-bets are made, except you can choose your number; you don't have to let the dice choose your numbers for you.** If you want to bet on 5, for example, simply toss your bet on the table while saying, "Five-dollar place-bet on 5." Make sure the dealer hears you; otherwise, your bet might be sitting in a box on the table layout where it could be construed as a different bet. The dealer positions all the place-bets for you. And, like the come-bets, they are located in the point-boxes based on your corresponding position at the table.

But place-bets come with a price. They don't pay true odds as the odds-bets do. They pay a little less. As you can see, the house percentage on place-bets for the 6 and 8 are not too bad. But place-bet percentages on the other point-numbers are higher than we would like.

BET	PAYS	SHOULD PAY	CASINO ADVANTAGE
Any 7	4 to 1	5 to 1	16.67%
Any Craps	7 to 1	8 to 1	11.1
11 (or 3)	15 to 1	17 to 1	11.1
2 (or 12)	30 to 1	35 to 1	13.89
Hard 6 (or 8)	9 to 1	10 to 1	9.1
Hard 4 (or 10)	7 to 1	8 to 1	11.1
Place 6 (or 8)	7 to 6	6 to 5	1.52
Place 5 (or 9)	7 to 5	3 to 2	4.0
Place 4 (or 10)	9 to 5	2 to 1	6.67

Remember when the shooter made that nice pass with a winner 4, "the hard way"? Well, the term *hardway* refers to yet another bet you can make, part of an assortment of bets all located in the center of the table, made and paid by the dealer handling the stick.

Hardways are simply the point-numbers made with matching numbers. Two 2s are a hard 4, two 3s are a hard 6, and so on. Although the percentages are even higher on these bets, they can provide for incredible short-term winnings. Hardways have been instrumental in several huge wins I've witnessed. One in particular, and the focus of a betting strategy we'll discuss later, cost an Atlantic City casino over half a million dollars in less than an hour's play. Hardways were pivotal in that remarkable success story. But, we must be realistic. Because of the higher percentages associated with these bets, they must be made judiciously.

Hardways win if the numbers are made in pairs (hard). If the numbers are made any other way (easy), or if a 7 is thrown, the bets lose. Risky? Sure is. **Good gambling is good timing.** If you time it right, and you follow my strategies, you can forget the bus and take a limo home. If your timing is off, or you devise your own "system," you might have to hitchhike.

To bet hardways, simply toss your bet to the dealer at the center of the table in charge of the stick, and announce your bet loud and clear, such as: "Five-dollar hard six." The boxes for all the hardway bets are a little different from the point-number boxes in that they represent the entire table, not just one end, so you'll have to mentally divide the box in half and then note the area of the box that would represent your position at the table. And keep an eye on your bet. Remember, the bet is literally tossed to the dealer. **The hardway bet, as with all bets placed by a dealer, is never handed to the dealer. It is tossed down on the table.** Yeah, I know, the chip rolls around and there's confusion sometimes, but that's a part of the game. The commotion, with chips flying everywhere, is just part of the fun! It's like standing on the floor of the New York Stock Exchange on a busy Friday afternoon. Trust me. When the game gets hot, and bets are pouring in from everywhere, it's fun!

There are many other bets you can make at the dice tables, but none of these bets are featured in the betting strategies that follow. So we're not going to discuss them here. You've got plenty to digest, anyhow.

If you want to learn about them later, pick up a copy of *All About Craps,* which will give you more of the basics. If you ever decide you want to learn even more about this exciting game, try *Conquer-*

ing Casino Craps. It goes beyond the basics and includes, for example, a fascinating discussion on "power shooters," skilled players who have found ways to manipulate the dice.

Neat Things To Know

Before we begin our betting strategies to beat this game, let me list a few things that will help you enjoy the game. Some of these items are an integral part of the rules and regs that have become traditional with most casinos. Unfortunately, with the spate of casino proliferation in the '90s, many new casinos have chosen to adopt their own rules. It's hard to say what is standard any longer, so always ask before you wager.

- The pass-line is also called the "front line." Some players simply call a pass-line bet a "line-bet"; an odds-bet is called "odds"; a point-number is called the "point." A come-bet that wins with a seven-out is called "last come."

- **Odds-bets and place-bets are off on the come-out, but hardways work.** Some players may elect to call their odds-bets and place-bets working. Many players, however, call their hardways off on the come-out.

- A dealer may call "no roll" while the dice are in motion. **A roll is automatically "no roll" if both dice do not land on the table layout.** (The "box" where the casino's chips are kept, and the "boat" where extra dice are kept, are not considered a part of the table layout.) All other rolls count, even if one die lands on top of the other, leans against the wall, or strikes a player.

- If a point-number rolls with a come-bet in the point-box *and* in the come simultaneously, and if both bets are the same wager (excluding odds), the bets do not move and are simply paid "off and on," meaning the player's winnings are placed beside the come-bet in the come.

- Place-bets on 6 or 8 must be made in multiples of six dollars, since the odds payoff is 7 to 6.

- Odds-bets on 5 or 9 at a single-odds table must be made in multiples of two dollars, since the odds payoff is 3 to 2.

- Never make a pass-line wager after the shooter has established a point. You are giving up the best part of the wager (the come-out) and getting down just at the time the casino gains the edge. Not too smart.

- Players may take down their place-bets, odds-bets, or hardways at any time while the bet is in doubt by saying, "Take all my bets down." Or, a specific bet(s) may be taken down. However, the odds-bet behind a pass-line wager must be picked up by the player. Unlike the other bets, it cannot simply be called off. Line-bets and come-bets must play out. Bets that can be taken down can be called off on just the next roll by saying, "All my bets are off this roll only." It is commonly done after a die lands on the floor, but it is just a silly superstition: Dice on the floor, seven at the door.

- The term *press* means to double the amount of your wager. The term *parlay* means to increase your wager by the amount of your winnings.

- Opposite sides of a die always total 7 (6 and 1, 5 and 2, 4 and 3).

- At a single-odds table, the odds-bet can be five times any divisible unit of the line-bet or come-bet for the points of 6 or 8; four times for the points of 5 or 9. For example, A $15 line-bet can take $25 odds for the points of 6 or 8; $20 for the points of 5 or 9.

- **Hold the dice with only one hand.** Never bring your other hand close to the dice. Can you guess why? Well, casino bosses are paranoid. They think every shooter is a sleight-of-hand artist. Just in case you're a magician by trade, leave the funny dice at home.

- **It's important that both dice actually bounce off the opposite wall.** Can you guess this one, too? Well, some cheaters know how to control the dice, but they don't hit the wall because that creates a random deflection. If you don't hit the wall, the bosses might think you're up to no good.

- Most players today *throw* the dice; they don't *roll* the dice. It's tough to roll them all the way to the wall, especially if you're standing at the far end of a table. But don't throw them too hard. The little buggers have very sharp edges, and have been known to draw blood from the knuckle of some unsuspecting player.

- When standing at a dice table, do not place your hands around the top edge of the table, or let your hands droop down over the table. I bet you can guess why.

CHAPTER 4

Craps:
Budget Gambling
Strategies

Most bets in the casino are a rapid win-or-lose affair. You bet, and within seconds you know whether or not you made the right choice. You will either have won, lost, or pushed (broken even).

But at the dice tables, all bets are not settled with the next roll of the dice. As you've now learned, pass-line bets, come-bets, and place-bets might take many rolls before a decision is reached. Although a craps table does provide bets that either win or lose on the next roll of the dice, these *one-roll bets,* as they are called, are not very good ones for you, at least not from a percentage point of view. In fact, none of these bets were discussed at length in the previous chapter, nor are they featured in any of the strategies that follow.

OK. So decisions will not fall with every roll of the dice, but you'll be in action; every roll of the dice *might* win or lose. This important component of our craps strategies helps you to develop patience in your play and reduce your exposure. It simply means that much of the time you are betting, you are in limbo, you are not cranking out decisions—bang, bang, bang. You are merely *awaiting* decisions. You are, in fact, *enjoying the anticipation* of a winning decision.

Optimum Betting

There's no question that the best bets to make are the low-percentage bets, especially if you're a frequent player, approaching or well into the long term. Sometimes it takes a good long while before percentages rear up and prove themselves... in honest-to-goodness dollars. I mean dollars won or dollars lost, but it's almost always dollars lost when one ventures into long-term exposure. It's not just true of craps, it's true of all the games with a negative expectation. Wouldn't you expect that? You wouldn't expect someone who plays much more often than you do to win more than you do, would you?

Seasoned dice players who can't turn back the clock know this all too well, so they only make pass-line bets and come-bets, and back them up with full double odds, or more if they can get it. They play the percentages. It's not the most exciting way to play, but it is the most effective.

The Four-Color Progressive Strategy For Craps

Playing the pass-line, along with a come-bet or two, and following the Four-Color Progressive Strategy detailed in Chapter 2 is the best attack on this fickle game. But there are some special rules and minor modifications to the rules that we need to list:

Special Rule 1. The amounts listed are for your pass-line or come-bet wager only. The amounts do not include odds. You must be prepared to make your additional odds-bets on point-numbers.

Incidentally, the progression is based on double odds. If you play triple-odds or greater, your increase in risk, particularly in the lower levels, outweighs the rewards. It's your call, but let me reiterate: **Double odds best fits the concept of *Budget Gambling*.**

Special Rule 2. Although a come-out loss always drops you down, no different from a point-number loss, betting amounts should remain static with come-out wins. Proceed up the progression only after a point-number win. There are exceptions to the latter, but as I learned from answering queries about my Power Betting Strategy, it is simply too hard to establish a regimen of do's and don'ts. Some players elect to go "same bet" three wins in a row on the come-out, and the next bet goes up. That's fine. In my case, however, I don't follow a particular rule; I simply go with my instincts.

57

Special Rule 3. It's the player's call whether or not to launch a come-bet or two. Personally, I rarely start a session with more than one come-bet in play. But if the come-bet hits, I might add another. In heated play, I would certainly have at least two come-bets working for me. Again, there can be no exacting rule.

But remember rule 8: If you win a pass-line bet in pre-play, make two come-bets, and win those, too, that's *not* three wins a row. Each bet must be treated separately. It's possible, with each bet treated independently, that you might have a lowly red chip sitting on the pass-line, while a come-bet has progressed up the ladder.

Incidentally, a come-bet that wins with a seven-out keeps its spot in the progression even though other bets would "drop down." If your "last come" was in the progression, keep the chips separate from others in your tray so that you can re-establish the bet on the next "roll for the point."

Betting Strategies For Place-Bets

Of the six place-bets that you can make, clearly the 6 and 8 are the points of choice for the astute craps player. The percentage on these bets is a low 1½ percent. Not as low as the pass-line with double odds, however, but significantly lower than the other point-numbers.

So here are some neat betting strategies for the 6 and 8 place-bets that include progressive, proposition, and parlay betting. **If you are a conservative player, pick *either* the 6 or 8. If you are a more aggressive player, bet *both* the 6 and 8.**

Remember that the rules of the Four-Color Progressive Strategy apply to all of the strategies that follow.

The 6 & 8 Straight Progressive Strategy

BET	WIN	GO TO	NET WIN	ACCUM WIN
6	7	same bet	1	1
6	7	same bet	7	8
6	7	12	1	9
12	14	18	8	17
18	21	24	15	32
24	28	30	22	54
30	35	60	5	59
60	70	90	40	99
90	105	120	75	174
120	140	180	80	254
180	210	240	150	404
240	280	300	220	624

Because 6s and 8s pay off at 7 to 6 odds, all your bets must be in multiples of $6. The chart shows the payoffs for all the hits up to $240. Try to get to the point where you can recall these payoffs by heart or at least figure them out in your head. It's easy. Do it the same way the dealers do. Simply divide your bet by 6 and multiply by 7.

This particular progression will be easier to remember anyhow, since the fourth level is the same as the second level... with a zero. Twelve dollars pays $14; $120 pays $140. The payoff for $60 is easy to remember for the same reason.

The reason the net win after the first win is only $1 is because you will eventually lose the $6 initial bet... in the sense that this progression, like all the others, plays to a loss. Technically, a drop-down wager should also be counted against winnings since it represents a new bet that will eventually lose. Hopefully, it will take a long time for it to happen, while you see lots of 6s or 8s parade by.

Some players have unilaterally chosen to adjust pre-play to only two wins for this particular strategy. I don't recommend it at all. You invest $6, you win $7; you go "same bet" with $6 and win another $7. You start the progression at $12 and lose that bet. Now count your winnings. It's easy. You started with $6 and you have $8 in "winnings." Eight minus 6 is 2. You just won $2. Do yourself a favor: Follow the strategy.

The 6 & 8 Straight Progressive Strategy With Cream

BET	CREAM	WIN	GO TO	NET WIN	ACCUM WIN
6		7	same bet	1	1
6		7	same bet	7	8
6		7	12	1	9
12	Add $5 Hardway	14	18	8	17
18		21	24	15	32
24	Press Hardway	28	30	22	54
30		35	60	5	59
60	Press Hardway	70	90	40	99
90		105	120	75	174
120	Press Hardway	140	180	80	254
180		210	240	150	404
240	Press Hardway	280	300	220	624

I like this one. It's the same as the 6 & 8 Straight Progressive Strategy, except I added a kicker. A proposition kicker. And when it's working, you'll be kicking the casino's ass.

The trick to making these hardway bets really pay off is to press them every time they hit. The payoff is 9 to 1, so the first time you hit one you'll pick up $45. Give the dealer $5 and you'll get two greenies in return ($50 for $5). Throw another $5 chip on the hardway and you'll be looking at a nice $90 payoff (that's right, give the dealer two $5 chips and you'll get a blackie in return... $100 for $10). Remember to always press your hardway after it hits.

The extra presses noted in the strategy (Press Hardway) are exactly that. No matter how much you have on the hardway, press it at that point in the progression. If you just hit the point with a hardway, and your next bet calls for an additional press, press it twice. You'll be risking only a small portion of your winnings if you follow the rules. The press, particularly when well into the progression, might mean considerable investment, but your winnings will be many times as considerable at that point. It's all part of the program.

If a hardway comes down with an easy number, go ahead and restore it for the next roll. Some players might find that a bit ambitious, but the hardways are the essence of this strategy. Remember, although the hardway may have lost with an easy number, that number won as a place-bet.

Regardless of where you are in the strategy when you see your first loss, hardway bets are not restored when you make your drop-down bet. If your drop-down bet takes you to $18 (or $12), for example, you will reboot the hardway at $5. Should the drop-down bet be $30 (or $24), for example, you start a hardway at $10 ($5 pressed). Simply follow the strategy. *Exit rules should protect you from losing a goodly portion of your winnings.* But if you are caught up in a lose-one, win-one scenario while high in the progression, you would be wise to exit early, even though the strategy will automatically be taking you down... eventually to preplay.

The 6 & 8 Press Strategy

BET	WIN	NEXT	NET WIN		ACCUM WIN
6	7	press	1		1
12	14	same bet	14	(15 for 1)	15
12	14	press	2		17
24	28	go to 30	22		39
30	35	press	5		44
60	70	same bet	70	(75 for 5)	114
60	70	press	10		
124					
120	140	same bet	140	(150 for 10)	264
120	140	press	20		284
240	280	same bet	280	(300 for 20)	564
240	280	go to 300	220		784
300	350	press	50		834

This unusual strategy really doesn't have a preplay, at least not in the sense that you need three wins in a row to get out. This is what I call a "take/press" strategy which makes it simple to remember. You take the first win; you press the next. Then take it, then press it again, and so on.

Dealers will usually catch on to what you're doing, They'll pay your take bets and press your next bet for you.

What's really neat about this strategy is its win potential compared to the 6 & 8 Straight Progressive Strategy. Note that this strategy gets stronger with the sixth win. Now look at the total of the accumulated wins in this strategy and the total of the wins in the other one. And finally, look at what would be the 13th betting level in both strategies. With this Press Strategy, you would be primed for a $700 payoff with $600 sitting in the box. With the Progressive Strategy, you would have only $300 ready to go. Both strategies have the same number of bets. Surprised?

But there is another side to it: This added aggressiveness of the Press Strategy will cost you more when you lose a bet. For example, a loss at the second level of the Progressive Strategy will result in a net win of $1. A loss at the second level of the Press Strategy will result in a net *loss* of $5.

There are some tricks to minimize lower-denomination chips in your payoffs. Take a win at $12, for example. It pays $14. Give the dealer $1 and you'll get three reds in exchange... $15 for $1. It works at $60, too. It pays $70. Give the dealer a red chip and you'll get three greenies in return... $75 for $5.

Oh, the reason why the $24 bet doesn't press, but goes to $30 instead, is to allow you to run up in those nice multiples of 30 and 60, and so on. The bets are easier to make, and the odds are easier to figure.

The 4 & 10 Parlay Press Strategy

BET	WIN	GO TO	NET WIN	ACCUM WIN
5	9	10	−1	−1
10	18	25 (1)	2	1
25	50	50 (2)	23	24
50	100	100 (5)	45	69
100	200	same bet (5)	195	264
100	200	300 (15)	−15	249
300	600	same bet (15)	585	834
300	600	900 (45)	−45	789
900	1800	same bet (90)	1710	2499
900	1800	2000*(100)	600	3099
2000	4000	same bet (100)	3900	6999

*Table limit

The number in parenthesis represents a "five-percent commission" that the casino charges to "buy" the 4 or 10 instead of place it. Buy-bets pay off at true odds of 2 to 1. The $5 and $10 bets that start the progression are place-bets and pay 9 to 5. The minimum commission the casino charges is $1 so it does not pay to make buy-bets until your wager is $25. Technically, the commission on a $25 bet should be $1.25, but there are no quarters at the tables. The casino settles for a dollar on a $25 bet and $2 on a $50 bet. It's about the only nice thing casinos do for players that I can think of.

I purposely moved to the $25 bet quickly so that we can start making some decent money while keeping our payoffs in nice, even multiples of chip denominations. The downside, of course, is in the rush to get there. It's not a question of patience; it's a question of probabilities. There are only three ways to make a 4 or a 10. There are six ways to make a 7.

I rest my case.

A Reminder

As you play and enjoy these strategies, remember that all of them are subject to the Four-Color rules found in Chapter 2. There are easy ways to remember the basics.

Here's the way I do it: Three to get in, three to drop down, two to get out.

Start each session with $40. If your stake drops to $20, the session ends.

Remember, too, that pre-play rules are for *both* the start of a session and a return to pre-play. Whenever you're in pre-play, it takes three in a row to get out.

My personal rule ends each betting chapter, so you might as well get used to it:

If you can't afford to lose it, don't bet it.

CHAPTER 5

Blackjack: Rules Of The Game

Beginners seem to get mixed signals when they start to learn how to play this game. They hear about how "professional counters" make a living at blackjack and so they get the idea that studying up on the game is like going to school to learn a trade, or maybe just a hobby... a profitable hobby.

Well, get that crazy notion out of your head. I'm going to tell you some things about blackjack that no other author will ever do for you. I'm not out to sell you an "advanced" book on blackjack, I don't have any tapes to peddle, no seminars to fill, no infomercials, no 800-numbers to call. And you won't find any ads at the back of this book for miracle counting strategies that can make you rich.

Because it's all bunk. And I simply won't be a party to such out-and-out pandering. I will, however, show you how you can have fun at this game, and work the percentages against you down to a pretty low number, even lower than the best bet at a craps table. And for whatever you'll want to do with this knowledge, please promise me that you will keep your job intact.

Now that we're clear on that, let's look at another side of the game that beginners see. They suspect that the game might be too complex to master, too complex to really have any fun with. They compare the game to chess in its degree of difficulty. And you know what? They're mostly right about that! But chess is fun, once you learn all the neat strategies. Chess is a highly competitive game that many people think appeals only to intellectuals. Well, that's bunk, too. Anyone can learn chess just as anyone can learn blackjack. And blackjack is a little easier.

Whether the game proves difficult for you to learn, or not, is entirely up to you and to the attitude you take toward it. **If you want easy, play slots. If you want a game with intellectual stimulus, play blackjack.** But remember, you don't have to be super-smart to play intelligently. Blackjack is just a casino game; it isn't rocket science.

The flip side to all this is the tendency of many beginners to think the game actually *is* easy. The arrogance of these players shows quickly. I can see it within seconds after I sit down to play. It would seem as if every table has at least a couple of players who think they have it all figured out,

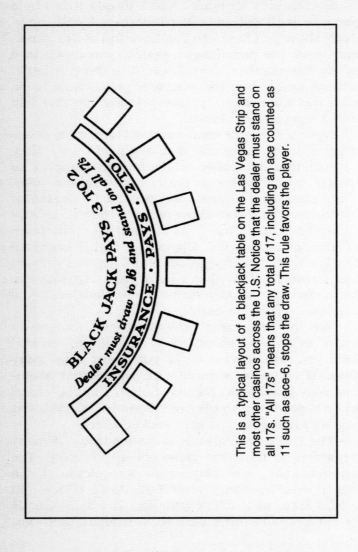

BLACK JACK PAYS 3 TO 2

Dealer must draw to 16 and stand on all 17s

INSURANCE · PAYS · 2 TO 1

This is a typical layout of a blackjack table on the Las Vegas Strip and most other casinos across the U.S. Notice that the dealer must stand on all 17s. "All 17s" means that any total of 17, including an ace counted as 11 such as ace-6, stops the draw. This rule favors the player.

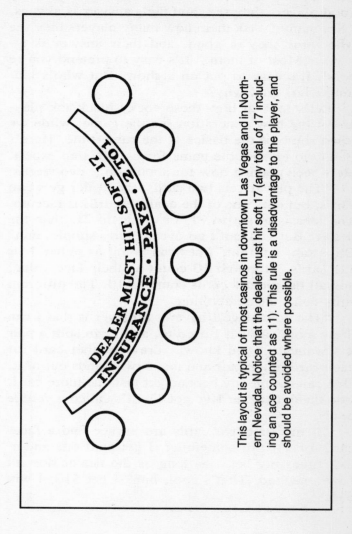

This layout is typical of most casinos in downtown Las Vegas and in Northern Nevada. Notice that the dealer must hit soft 17 (any total of 17 including an ace counted as 11). This rule is a disadvantage to the player, and should be avoided where possible.

but they haven't a clue. Ask the dealers how many good players they see, and their answer is always, "Not many." Ask them how many players they see who *think* they're good, and their answer is always, "Most of them." It's easy to pretend you're good. It's easy to put on a show. But who's kidding who? And why?

Let's look at how these cocky blackjack players of the new generation see the game, while we learn some of the basics at the same time. Here's Benny to explain the game for us. He's an expert. He's been playing now for about, oh... two weeks.

"The player gets two cards; the dealer gets two cards, but only one of the dealer's cards is face up. The idea is to get to 21, or closer to 21, than the dealer. But you can't go over. Pretty simple, huh? Oh, yeah, I forgot. Aces can count as either 1 or 11; cards 2 through 10 count as their face value; and all the picture cards count as 10. The different suits don't mean anything.

"The advantage I have as a player is that I can draw more cards if I need to, and I can split a pair if I want to... you know... draw another card for each card in the pair and make two hands out of it. Or I can double my bet and get just one more card. I do that whenever I've got 11. It's called a *double down*.

"If my first two cards are an ace and a face-card, or a 10 of something, I get paid one-and-a-half times my bet... as long as the dealer doesn't have one, too. That's cool, huh? I bet $10; I win $15.

"Don't tell anybody, but I count the cards. I keep track of the 10s and face-cards, and I keep a side-count of aces. Those are all good cards for me. When there's a surplus of these cards left in the deck, I bet really big!

"Another big plus for me, as a player, is that the dealer has to draw to make at least 17. The dealer is forced to do that. Let's say the dealer has a 10 and a 5. That's 15. By rule, the dealer's gotta draw another card. Anything over a 6 will bust that hand. A bust means I win. Remember, I said you can't go over 21. And get this: I don't have to draw if I don't want to. That's what's really neat about this game. If I don't have a good hand, I just sit back and hope the dealer busts!"

Thank you, Benny. You should go write a book or something.

Now let's look at what Benny *didn't* tell us.

It's true that you have a lot of options as a blackjack player, and they are all advantages that you must use. But you also have a huge *dis*advantage that is nearly insurmountable: You must draw first! It's worth nearly seven percent to the house. If the dealer drew first, then... yes, we could all make a living at this game.

By rating all the advantages you have, just as Benny listed them, it's possible to overcome that nasty seven-percent house edge, if—and this is a big if—the game rules are player-friendly. It's even possible for you to pick up a slight—and that's *very* slight—edge by keeping track of the played cards, called *card-counting*.

Another thing our "expert" didn't tell us about is what's collectively termed *casino countermeasures*. You didn't think you could just walk up, sit down, count the cards, take all the casino's money, and walk out the door... day in, day out... did you? You really don't think casinos are run by a bunch of stupids, do you? Later on, in a brief section on card-counting, I'll list all the casino countermeasures so you can best prepare yourself by learning what not to do to give yourself away.

Benny also misled us on one important point: He said, "The idea of the game is to get to 21, or closer to 21, than the dealer." But that's not exactly true. *The idea of the game is to beat the dealer, which is certainly not the same as trying to get closest to 21 without going over*. It's a popular fallacy, and is probably the reason for the most common fault of beginners: drawing when they should stand pat.

Can you guess the second most common fault of rank beginners? It's the exact opposite action: They *don't* draw when they *should* draw. They rely too heavily on the dealer's likelihood of busting.

Drawing or standing, splitting or doubling... you simply must know the right moves. For every player/dealer hand combination, there *is* a right move. It's called *basic strategy*... a time-tested, computer-proven set of rules for player options developed decades ago, and it works like a charm, but you have to work, too. It does take some work, but it takes the *guess*work out of the game.

To alleviate your fear that you will have to memorize a chart on a par with Lincoln's

Gettysburg Address, let me tell you here and now that I have reproduced a complete chart of all the possible player-hand and dealer up-card combinations, which appears following the conclusion of this section of the chapter. The same chart is reproduced in color at the front of *Budget Gambling.* Tear it out and take it with you when you play.

In addition, I've provided segments of this chart throughout the next few pages, which will help you as we discuss these specific parts of the strategy.

Let's start our discussion of basic strategy with the option that comes into play most often:

Hitting And Standing

To signal a hit (draw another card), the casino prefers that you bring your hand toward you in a scooping motion. I prefer to simply point at the cards, actually touching the table with my finger about two to three inches from the cards.

If you wish to stand (no draw), the casino wants you to move your hand in a horizontal motion, as if you're wiping a piece of glass above the table. However, it's been my experience that this motion can easily be confused with the opposite signal, especially if a player is particularly sloppy with the motions. I prefer to simply put out my hand, palm toward the dealer, as if to indicate "stop." Try my way.

Hit-Or-Stand Strategy For Stiffs

PLAYER'S HARD HAND	DEALER'S UP-CARD									
	2	3	4	5	6	7	8	9	10	A
16										
15										
14	S	T	A	N	D		H	I	T	
13										
12	H	I	T							

A player's hand that could bust with a 10-value card is called a "stiff."

The term *hard* in this chart means the hands do not include an ace.

The chart also assumes the hands 12, 14, and 16 are not paired, such as 8-8 for 16.

Always hit a stiff when the dealer has a 7 or higher. Remember it as 7-UP and you'll never forget it.

Always stand on a stiff when the dealer has a 6 or less showing, with the exception of 12.

Always stand on 17 or better.

Always draw a card on 11 or less. You might actually double down or split, depending on the card values, but at the very least, you'll always hit it.

Incidentally, this strategy applies not only to your first two cards, but to your changing hand as you draw more cards. For example, if your original hand was 13 against the dealer's 10, you must draw. If you drew a 3, your hand is now 16. You must draw again. You must continue to draw until you have 17 or higher.

Splitting

Another important option for you is to split identical cards in your original hand, such as a pair of 8s. The chart that follows will show you when to split, and when not to.

To indicate a split to the dealer, simply place an additional bet of the same size within the betting circle directly beside (not on top of) your original wager. You must tell the dealer that you wish to split. This is one of only two times when a verbal signal is required. Otherwise, the action could, in some cases, be construed as a double down, which we'll talk about next.

The dealer will deliver two more cards, one to each card split, in effect, making two new hands for you. Each hand will be subject to all the other player options, but you must act on one hand first and complete it before you act on the other.

Should you receive another identical card, some casinos will allow you to re-split the new pair. Most casinos, however, do not allow the re-splitting of aces. To make matters worse, many casinos will not allow you to draw after splitting aces.

Splitting Strategy

PLAYER'S HAND	DEALER'S UP-CARD									
	2	3	4	5	6	7	8	9	10	A
A-A			S	P	L	I	T			
10-10			S	T	A	N	D			
9-9										
8-8			S	P	L	I	T			
7-7										
6-6							H	I	T	
5-5		D	O	U	B	L	E			
4-4							H	I	T	
3-3			S	P	L	I	T			
2-2										

Here's how to remember our splitting strategy: Always split aces and 8s. Never split 10s, 5s, and 4s.

Treat 5-5 as 10 and follow the double-down rule that follows.

Split 9s when the dealer has 9 or less, split 7s when the dealer has 7 or less, and split 6s when the dealer has 6 or less.

Only split 2s and 3s when the dealer's up-card is a 4, 5, 6, or 7.

Doubling Down

This option figures prominently in your goal of reducing the house percentage against you. A double down is allowed on your first two cards (or in some cases, the first two cards following a split). To do this, simply place an additional bet of the same size or less within the betting circle directly beside (not on top of) your original wager. This is the other of the two times when a verbal signal is recommended. Otherwise, the action could, in the case of 5-5 or 4-4, be construed as a split.

Obviously, the best time to double down is when you have a hand-total of 10 or 11 and the dealer's up-card is 6 or less. But there are times when doubling on 9 and on certain "soft" hands are recommended. We'll talk about soft hands next.

The problem with double downs is that many casinos restrict this valuable player option to only 10 or 11. You can't double down on 9, you can't double down on 4-4, you can't double down on a soft 17, and you can't double down after you split.

Double Down Strategy For Hard Hands

PLAYER'S HARD HAND	DEALER'S UP-CARD									
	2	3	4	5	6	7	8	9	10	A
11			D	O	U	B	L	E		
10			D	O	W	N				
9						H	I	T		

The variations in rules for double downs and splits are perhaps the best reasons why you must shop for the very best playing conditions.

Always double down on 11 regardless of the dealer's up-card.

Doubling on 10 is restricted to a dealer's up-card of 9 or lower.

Only double on 9 if the dealer's up-card is 3, 4, 5, or 6.

Yes, there are times when you double on 8, but only if you're counting the cards, which we'll talk about later.

Soft Hands

Any hand that includes an ace has two values: a soft value and a hard value. If your hand is an ace-6, the soft value is 17 (counting the ace as 11), the hard value is 7 (counting the ace as 1).

As you study the chart that follows, it's important to remember that a soft hand, such as a soft 17, will not bust. A 10-value card will simply make the soft 17 hard.

Refer back to the table charts at the top of this chapter. On the strip in Las Vegas and in most other major casinos across the country, the dealer is required to *draw to 16 and stand on all 17s*. But in much of Northern Nevada, downtown Las Vegas, and some Indian casinos, the rule is different, requiring the dealer to hit a soft 17. It's a nasty ploy, and definitely a disadvantage to you.

Look on the table layout before you play. It should clearly state, "The dealer must draw to 16 and stand on *all* 17s." Much better!

Soft-Hand Strategy

PLAYER'S SOFT HAND	DEALER'S UP-CARD									
	2	3	4	5	6	7	8	9	10	A
A-9 (20)			S	T	A	N	D			
A-8 (19)										
A-7 (18)				D						
A-6 (17)				O						
A-5 (16)	H			U						
A-4 (15)	I			B			H	I	T	
A-3 (14)	T			L						
A-2 (13)				E						

Always stand on a soft 19 and 20. They represent good hands, regardless of the dealer's up-card.

Always double down (if you can) on a soft 13 through 18 when the dealer has a 4, 5, or 6 showing.

A soft 18 is the most difficult to remember because there are three options: Always double down on a soft 18 when the dealer is showing a 4, 5, or 6... and hit it when the dealer is showing a 9, 10, or ace. Otherwise, stand.

On the following page is a chart that combines all the previous charts into one. Sure, you can use the chart while at the table, but it looks a lot more pro to make your moves from memory. You'll find that after several hours of play, many of the options will become routine for you. It's like any-

Blackjack Basic Strategy

PLAYER HAND	DEALER UP-CARD									
	2	3	4	5	6	7	8	9	10	A
8	H	H	H	H	H	H	H	H	H	H
9	H	D	D	D	D	H	H	H	H	H
10	D	D	D	D	D	D	D	D	H	H
11	D	D	D	D	D	D	D	D	D	D
12	H	H	S	S	S	H	H	H	H	H
13	S	S	S	S	S	H	H	H	H	H
14	S	S	S	S	S	H	H	H	H	H
15	S	S	S	S	S	H	H	H	H	H
16	S	S	S	S	S	H	H	H	H	H
A-2	H	H	D	D	D	H	H	H	H	H
A-3	H	H	D	D	D	H	H	H	H	H
A-4	H	H	D	D	D	H	H	H	H	H
A-5	H	H	D	D	D	H	H	H	H	H
A-6	H	H	D	D	D	H	H	H	H	H
A-7	S	S	D	D	D	S	S	H	H	H
A-8	S	S	S	S	S	S	S	S	S	S
A-9	S	S	S	S	S	S	S	S	S	S
2-2	H	H	SP	SP	SP	SP	H	H	H	H
3-3	H	H	SP	SP	SP	SP	H	H	H	H
4-4	H	H	H	H	H	H	H	H	H	H
5-5	D	D	D	D	D	D	D	D	H	H
6-6	SP	SP	SP	SP	SP	H	H	H	H	H
7-7	SP	SP	SP	SP	SP	SP	H	H	H	H
8-8	SP	SP	SP	SP	SP	SP	SP	SP	SP	SP
9-9	SP	SP	SP	SP	SP	SP	SP	SP	S	S
10-10	S	S	S	S	S	S	S	S	S	S
A-A	SP	SP	SP	SP	SP	SP	SP	SP	SP	SP

| H=HIT | S=STAND | D=DOUBLE | SP=SPLIT |

thing else. But if you don't play frequently, carry the strategy card with you to help ensure that you are playing basic strategy flawlessly.

There have only been a few cases reported to me where strategy cards were not allowed at the tables. Upon investigation, I learned that the casinos had banned the cards because their use slowed the pace of the game. Other players, apparently, were complaining. So, to avoid any embarrassment, ask a dealer or pit boss before you sit down if the strategy cards are OK to use.

The next section of this chapter takes us to card-counting. I'm going to show you two strategies that will help you win more when you win, and lose less when you lose, by keeping track of the cards. But I can't provide a pocket-sized card for you to keep with you. Any cards or equipment, or anything that even remotely involves card-counting, is a no-no at the tables. So, as you'll soon see, I've purposely simplified the strategies to make them easier for you to remember. That's right, you'll have to store your card-counting strategy... and use it, all in your head.

By the way, I decided to include strategies on card-counting in this chapter instead of the more logical "strategies" chapter that follows because card-counting is a basic component of the game, in the same way that basic strategy is basic to the game. An introductory discussion of card-carding definitely belongs in "rules of the game."

Card-Counting

It's easier to understand the principle behind card-counting if we go back many years to when Nevada casinos routinely dealt the game from a single deck. In those years, smart players knew that certain cards were of greater benefit to the player than to the dealer. And, unlike the multiple-deck shoes (a device that holds more than one deck) in today's casino, having to keep track of the cards from only one deck was much easier. It really didn't take long for shrewd players to catch on; they realized that they should vary their betting as they noted particular cards coming out of the deck. As played cards were removed from the deck, the composition of the remaining deck was altered.

The ace is the obvious example. Coupled with a 10-value card, it pays 3 to 2 as a blackjack for the player, but only loses at even money if the dealer wins with a blackjack. If players noticed that no aces had been played after, say, half of the deck was exhausted, the fact that four aces were left in only half of the deck was certainly a plus for them. The composition of the remaining deck had been altered to the player's favor. It was no longer a random distribution. Instead of two aces remaining to be played, as would be the expected norm halfway through the deck, there were now four aces left.

But the ace is certainly not the only card worth tracking. Ten-value cards are a real plus for the players, too. They are often a vital card in a double down or split; they pair up with an ace for a blackjack; and they contribute to a dealer bust when

82

hitting a stiff. But they contribute to a player's bust, too, you counter. And that's right, but you're forgetting something: A player does not always hit a stiff; whereas, the rules of the game require a dealer to always draw to 17.

So, what do you suppose we can make of all the little cards, such as 2, 3, 4, 5, and 6? Are these cards good for the player? No, the little cards favor the dealer, and you can probably guess why. If a 10-value card busts a dealer's stiff, what do you suppose the little cards do? Absolutely, they make a dealer's stiff pat (a standing hand). When the dealer turns over the hole-card and shows 15, for example, any of the little cards will make the dealer's hand pat.

These little cards also work against a player's double down. When you double down on 11, you're looking for a 10-value card, not a 4 or 5. Same goes for a player split. When you split 8s, for example, 10-value cards give you 18; a 4 or 5 present you with a stiff.

Of all the little cards, the 4 and 5 are the worst cards for the player. The 7, 8, and 9 are generally regarded as neutral, although the 8 is the only card among them that actually sits on the fence. The 7 leans to the dealer, the 9 leans to the player.

Now you can see that the concept behind card-counting is easy. Practicing it, however, is not.

The Simple Point-Count

Here's the easiest—and not surprisingly, the most popular—card-counting strategy. If you study the chart for a moment, you'll quickly see the reasoning behind it. The small cards are counted as "plus 1" as they are seen emerging from the deck; the ace and 10-value cards are counted as "minus 1."

PLUS (COUNT +1)					MINUS (COUNT −1)				
2	3	4	5	6	7	8	9	10	A
1	1	1	1	1	0	0	0	1	1

Most beginners have trouble thinking of the good cards in terms of a minus number. But that's the right way to do it because you are counting these good cards as they are removed from the deck. They are gone; you will not be able to use their advantage. What you are actually counting are negative conditions. Think of it the same way as if you're counting all the red and black jelly-beans that someone is taking out of a candy dish. The more that are taken out, the more of a negative condition remains for you... I mean, who wants to eat the orange and yellow ones?

That's right. The orange and yellow jelly-beans are like the little cards in the deck. And, as they are played, it's a positive situation for you. The more of them taken out, the higher the ratio of the good cards that are left for *you*!

The High-Ace Point Count

Before you get comfy with the Simple Point-Count Strategy, I'm going to show you another one that's more powerful. In retail, this is called "selling up." I'm going to take you from the four-door coupe to the sports car you really want without charging you a cent more. Such a deal!

The High-Ace Point Count contains two basic changes that help to rectify what appears to be a flaw in the Simple Point-Count Strategy. Most sharp beginners pick up on it right away. Did you catch it, too? Well, it's not as big a deal as it looks, but there is definitely some severe "rounding off" if we are only to use "minus 1" and "plus 1" values. A 2 or 3, for example, is less of a detriment to you than a 4 or 5, so technically we should not apply the same "plus 1" value to each of these cards. By the same token, the ace is a more important card to you than the 10-value card, yet both values are treated as "minus 1."

In spite of these apparent discrepancies, the Simple Point-Count Strategy has been used successfully for decades. It was regarded as one of the most simple, yet effective, strategies when card-counting was first developing, and remains widely used even to this day.

To offer up a strategy with each card being assigned its true relative value would be in opposition to the theme of *Budget Gambling*. The burden of practicing such a complex strategy, let alone remembering the many different values, would take the fun out of playing blackjack for the great majority of readers.

A better solution is The High-Ace Point Count whereby we can use only three counting values: "plus 1," "minus 1," and minus 2." I've refined this proven strategy only slightly to make it easier for you to use.

PLUS (COUNT +1)						MINUS*			
2	3	4	5	6	7	8	9	10	A
1	1	1	1	1	1	0	0	1	2

*COUNT −1 FOR 10-VALUE CARDS; COUNT −2 FOR ACES

What's remarkable about such a subtle change from the Simple Point-Count Strategy is that the overall effects of adding only one value (special to the ace), and adding one additional card to count as a little one (7), have greatly stabilized the other variations in card values for which we identified but did not account for. How wondrous! The end result is a powerful counting strategy that I call the High-Ace Point-Count.

Incidentally, as you practice your counting skills at home, I'm sure you'll quickly see that both counting strategies I've taught you can be tested for your accuracy. Since both strategies are a "balanced" point-count design, you should always end at "0" when you have counted the last card.

How To Use The Strategies

Whether you choose the easier Simple Point-Count or the more powerful High-Ace Point-Count, **the advantages of the strategies are realized in two ways: in the way you bet and in the way you alter basic strategy.**

As you see the cards played, mentally count the cards and let your "count" determine the size of your bet. If, for example, your count reaches "minus 5," you should bet at the table minimum because the deck is running significantly against you. In a typical six- or eight-deck game, many players elect to quit playing when their count reaches "minus 6," especially if it's early in the shuffle. Why wait around for a new shuffle? Why play with a negative expectation when you know that a positive expectation is yours for the finding?

When you do find yourself with a plus count, say "plus 6" or "plus 7," that's the time to increase your bet size. But, unlike the way most gaming authors recommend, I urge you not to make sudden, large increases in your bet. That only draws the attention of the pit bosses who are in charge of protecting the game *for the house!* Don't give yourself away.

A $5 bettor should increase the wager to $15; that's called a "spread of three" (increasing your bet three times). Although I've even recommended spreads of five in earlier writings, I'm better experienced at pulling this off than you might be. Of course, if you're a red-chip bettor, it's not likely that you'll draw the ire of many pit bosses. They're looking for the green- and black-chip bettors who pose a bigger threat to the house. Still, you should be on guard. The big bet-spread is the one obvious give-away of card-counters.

The other advantage of card-counting allows you to make changes in basic strategy based on your count. Let's use the same counts that we talked about in determining your bet structuring. If your count reaches "minus 5," telling you that the rate of removal of good cards has accelerated, you will want to think twice before you double down on 11. You might even want to hit 14 versus the dealer's 6, even though basic strategy tells you to stand.

If your count runs into positive territory, however, all the way to "plus 7," for example, a double down on 8 might be a good decision. Of course, you'll only be able to do that if the casino allows you to double down on *any two cards*. Knowing that there are fewer little cards left than should be, you would be wise to stand on 12 regardless of the dealer's up-card.

Casino Countermeasures

If a pit boss suspects you of counting, and if you're into a nice run, it's possible that the dealer will be told to "shuffle up," which means making a premature shuffle that will wipe out your positive count, not to mention infuriate the other players at the table.

The dealer may also be instructed to "burn" more cards (cards not to be played) by placing the cut-card farther from the end of the decks. Instead of burning one deck of a six-deck shoe, perhaps the cut-card penetration will kill two decks. The benefits of card-counting are greatly reduced as more cards are taken out of play.

What I've noticed to be the most common action, and what I believe to be the most effective, is nothing more than "pressure" from the bosses. Maybe two bosses. They'll watch every move you make. They'll whisper to each other as they stare you down. They'll go to the phones and talk to someone, and you know they're talking about you. Most likely, the person at the other end of the phone conversation is a surveillance person who will be asked to focus the camera on you, zoom in, and start taping.

In some venues, you may be asked to leave. This drastic action happens far fewer times than you might have heard.

The Rewards Of Card-Counting

Blackjack is a game of constantly changing expectation, but only a counter can identify it. For non-counters, the game is essentially random, with a slight negative edge for a typical basic-strategy player.

But just exactly how big a deal is all this? Is it worth the effort to master card-counting? I guess it depends on whether or not you are going to be a frequent player or just a casual, once- or twice-a-year player. And it depends on whether or not you find the challenge of developing a skill as a rewarding accomplishment. And it also depends on just exactly how "rewarding" it can be. That is really the key question to ask. So ask me.

Here's my answer: Go get a deck of cards and remove all the 4s and 5s. Remember I told you that these two card-values are the worst offenders of all. With all the 4s and 5s removed from the deck, a rank beginner would think that the remaining deck construction should prove to be a virtual lock for winning. But is it? Find out yourself.

Go through the deck several times. Count the number of winning and losing hands, and remember to count a blackjack as one-and-one-half wins. A winning double down or split counts as two wins. If you go through this "stacked" deck ten times, you should come out ahead six times, winning by three to five units. Your results may vary because we are only making a short-term test. But the results will tell you two things:

For one, this extremely positive deck—one that you would never find in actual play unless the first eight cards dealt were 4s and 5s—does not guarantee you anything. Nothing. You might even lose. But, after doing this memorable exercise, you'll probably realize that over the long term the edge is distinctly there. It's more subtle than you probably expected, so it will take more hands before it proves itself. For most blackjack players, however, it will take more hands than they have the patience for.

And something else that you should realize by now is that the percentage of time when you do have a positive count is not as frequent as you might have imagined. Most of the time, you are playing in a neutral or negative environment. The times when your count moves wildly to the plus side are rare, indeed. And you've just learned that even when the plus side is at a maximum, the results may be surprising in the short term.

Neat Things To Know

- Don't be confused by the term *blackjack*. An ace and *any* 10-value card is a blackjack. You should get one about once in every 22 hands.

- The four suits of cards have no significance in blackjack.

- The game was originally called "21" and many casinos today still use that name.

- In the days before modern gaming, a blackjack was an ace and a jack of clubs or spades, and it paid 10 to 1. Today, there are no casinos that offer this rule, other than on rare occasion as a special promotion.

- Which reminds me. As the number of casinos increase, and the competition for players becomes more intense, you'll find promotions of this sort that must be looked at with skepticism. As an example, some casinos offer a 2 to 1 payoff for a winning hand of 7-7-7. But, like so many other "bonus payoffs," what looks like a great deal for you might be offered only to mask an otherwise unfavorable set of *other* rules... more important rules, like doubling on any two cards, or doubling after you split. Check *all* the rules carefully before you play.

- **Never touch the cards.** Most all casinos today deal the cards face-up, relying solely on hand signals to convey your instructions to the dealer. Similarly, **never touch your bet until the bet has been settled.**

CHAPTER 6

Blackjack:
Budget Gambling
Strategies

Of all the casino games, blackjack stands out in more ways that one.

You now know that it's a game of varying expectation, and that only a card-counter can detect these variations. Such an intriguing factor certainly sets it apart from all the other games.

And you also now know that a universally accepted "basic strategy" has been devised to make every decision "by the book." No pondering. No guessing. Every possible hand combination has a right or wrong action. Sometimes the right action is the wrong action, and the wrong action is the right action, but, over time, the strategy will always bear out. No other casino game offers such impressive credentials for success.

But blackjack has another unique honor, and a rather dubious one at that: It is rarely played with solid, *safe* betting strategies. That's right. Some of the worst, if not *the* worst, betting mistakes are found at the blackjack tables. Don't believe me? Ask any dealer. You'll hear that the most reckless, unorganized, illogical betting is to be found there. Not at the dice tables, as most players would guess, and not at the roulette tables, either. Blackjack gets the nod as the table that cries out for discipline, for common sense, and, yes, for sanity in some cases.

Even dice dealers know this. Says one dealer, "I can tell which players are former blackjack players, and we're getting a lot of them lately. They go crazy over here."

Why? Because they went "crazy" over there!

A little bit of "crazy" at the blackjack tables translates into a lot of "crazy" at the dice tables. Indeed. Craps might offer ten times odds, but it's also ten times crazy, and you can get there ten times faster. I think it's fair to say that if you're not in complete control as a blackjack player, your steering wheel is going to come off as you race around a craps table.

But let's get back to the point at hand: Why do blackjack players, particularly the younger breed, have such problems with a game that is supposed to be beatable? I mean, they're not only defying the game's image, they're putting it in jeopardy. Its reputation is at stake! Blackjack has long been recognized as a skill game that can be beaten over

the long term. Then why isn't it beaten? And believe me, it isn't beaten very often.

Think about it. Here we have a game that offers
the chance to actually play with a positive expectation... a player's edge! And it gets you there in the
most unusual how-to fashion by actually telling you
what to do: Hit, stand, double, whatever. This game
is almost too good to be true.

And that's part of the problem. Hear me out on
this one. There is such a positive expectation associated with blackjack... so positive... that good players are actually embarrassed to lose. And it's the
way they lose... their reaction to losing... that sets
the stage for at least one of our answers.

You would expect the more conservative players to be sitting at a blackjack table, right? I don't
mean geeks and nerds necessarily, but the more
serious players. Blackjack is even regarded by casino executives as an introvert's game. (All the
extroverts, I guess, are whooping it up at the dice
tables.) Blackjack players have that smug look of
poker players. That look of invincibility that usually
doesn't mean much to other poker players because
everyone wears it. Really now... who would want
to look vulnerable at a poker table? But we don't
dare compare blackjack players to poker players,
either. That would insult poker players.

Armed with the most powerful weapons, blackjack players are out to show their stuff. When they
win, the script is played out as it's written: the
typical Hollywood ending. But when they lose,
watch out! It's the greatest paradox in the casino.

And I consider this phenomenon to be the most critical element of the game. Hear me out again:

I don't care how good your basic strategy is. I don't care how good you are at card-counting. If you can't accept a loss, if you don't know how to lose, you'll never know how to win.

The most important strategy of all is not card-counting; it is not basic strategy; it is basic *discipline*.

Here's a true story that will make the point abundantly clear:

If You Can Build it, You Can Tear It Down

Woody had earned a reputation as a very good blackjack player. He won a few big tournaments, made a name for himself, and would eventually write for a gaming newsletter I published many years ago.

The last time I saw him, he was not playing up to his image. In fact, he was playing so poorly that I questioned the wisdom of even keeping his column running in the newsletter.

We met at the Tropicana, where, at the time, the casino was dealing a decent game. He had already played for a couple of days before I arrived, and he was upside down over a thousand dollars. Kind of surprised me.

He told me all about it over breakfast the next morning. "John, you wouldn't believe it. I was down a thousand after the first day. I was so upset with myself I couldn't sleep. I thought about leaving early, but I wanted to see you. I've never felt this depressed about my game. Ever felt the same way?"

"Umm, not exactly."

"Well, let me tell you. The next day I lost another thousand. Down two big ones. Can you believe it? I'm slamming doors, throwing stuff around, I'm so angry with myself I don't know what to do. So, instead of going to bed early... get this... I decided to try it again. I'm back at the same table, same dealer, and I caught a great streak. I won the thousand back! I go up to my room and I'm in ecstasy! I'm elated!"

"Yeah, but you were right back to where you were when you were so depressed the first time."

"I know. Weird, isn't it? I'm down a thousand and I feel rotten. I lose another thousand, win it back, and I feel great! Go figure."

"I don't know, Woody. I think this game is starting to mess with your mind. You want to try it again? Let me finish my coffee and we'll give it a go, but let's go easy."

As I played beside him, I couldn't help but notice his tendency to try to force the cards. It's a term I coined many years ago that describes the habit of many players to try to *force* good cards by betting heavy. It makes no sense. But people do it all the time.

As a counter, Woody knew the right time to bet heavy, but I was playing too, and I could count darn near as well as he could. I didn't find any exceptional shoes (a shuffle's worth of hands) during the entire morning we played. Yet Woody would occasionally throw out a stack of green as if

the cards were in the black. The term *black* incidentally, was part of a code Woody and I often
used so we could talk during play about the count,
without the dealer getting too suspicious. *Black*
meant we were in a positive count. *Red* meant we
were in the negative. *Midnight* and *blood* were the
extremes. Bloody obviously meant bad, and midnight was good.

We never reached midnight; never came close.
But we were well in the red a few times, and that's
another thing that surprised me. A good card-
counter is a table-hopper. When the cards turn red,
you move on. Makes sense, doesn't it? But Woody
just stayed... and stayed. He was so settled in, and
so *un*settled, that he wanted to prove to himself, I
guess, that he could win at that table. That *doesn't*
make sense. No sense at all.

After a break for lunch, we went back to the
casino to play again. I had tried to talk him into
going downtown where we could find several good
games. At the time, I had always believed there
were more options for blackjack players downtown,
although that's certainly not true today. There was
really no place to walk to from the Trop in those
days, other than the Marina. So, in a sense, we
felt somewhat isolated. The only table with two
adjacent spots open was that same table we had
left just an hour or so earlier. I told Woody I flat-
out refused to play there. He nodded, and followed
me out the door to get my rental car.

I wanted to stop at the Castaways (long since
gone) on the way downtown so we took my car
instead of his. But the bigger reason was I wanted

to drive. I wanted to control exactly where we were going to go. And make sure we got there.

I pulled into the Castaways and parked just a few yards from the door. Hard to believe today, but in those years, you could actually pull up, park your car, and walk into most casinos. Woody followed me in and waited while I cashed a winning sports ticket from my previous trip out there. I didn't have time to cash it after the game because I had a flight to catch early that next morning, as I recall. I'm always uncomfortable holding onto tickets, whether from the race book or the sports book. The time limit to cash them varies from one casino to another, and I was always paranoid I would eventually wait too long with one. I never liked the idea of mailing them in.

Anyhow, while I was standing in line, I ran into a friend of mine. We talked for a few minutes and then I wanted to introduce him to Woody. But Woody was gone. He wasn't in the sports book; he was in the casino. I knew exactly where to find him. The blackjack pit had few takers. Woody was easy to spot.

"Woody, what the hell are you doing? You know this game isn't any good here. You can't even re-split aces." The casino had finally gone the way of most of the other Strip hotels and toughened the rules. And here was Woody, playing under conditions that even a novice would avoid. We were on our way to find a better game, but Woody couldn't wait. It was clear to me now. Woody had confused "playing" with "winning." He wasn't looking to win, he was looking to play.

A great counter, a threat to casinos, as I re-membered him. All gone now. He didn't even have the discipline to shop for the best playing condi-tions. And that's something I always enjoyed do-ing during my many trips to that desert oasis. First, I would call my buddies and find out where the best games were. The rules were always changing. It meant that a good player would have to stalk. It became an integral part of the game. But it re-quired patience. Something that Woody apparently had left behind.

He was so good at the game that it finally caught up with him. He thought he was so good that he could win under any circumstances.

No, he couldn't. You can't, either.

Blackjack Express

Another player destroyer that we should iden-tify is probably not the casino's fault, either. Like the arrogance of those "I'm bigger than the game" players we just talked about, *the anxiety factor,* as I like to call it, is equally detrimental. I like play-ers to have an anxiety to win. I just don't like an anxiety to play. Play, play, play.

I touched upon this briefly in the first chapter. Players like "quick." They want to play quickly and win quickly. It's the antithesis of patience. And what better table-game to deliver the decisions, fast and furious, than blackjack.

Most beginners would guess that craps is the fast game. But no, it really isn't. In our third chap-ter about craps, we learned that the game has a fast way about it, but the decisions aren't fast. In fact, sometimes they're downright slow. What makes the game appear fast is the multitude of bets. But no players in their right mind are betting them all! Maybe it just seems that way to casual observers.

Indeed, craps doesn't get the prize for fast decisions. No. It's blackjack, at least it does among the table-games covered in this book. Technically, baccarat would get the nod, but that game has a too-high minimum bet to be considered for *Budget Gambling*. If we count *all* the games, slot machines provide the fastest decisions of all. And we'll cover how to deal with that problem in a later chapter on slots.

Did you know there's a decision nearly every minute at a blackjack table? It can be more or less, depending on how many players are at a table, but believe me, one of the attractions of the game is speed. It's a sign of the times, I guess. Today's young players are simply too anxious to find out if they have won or lost.

Some card-counters I've talked to today take a different tack to the issue of game speed than did their earlier counterparts. I'll side with the counters who pioneered the concept many years ago. I'm from the old school, too, where I learned that I must set my own pace. Old school or new school, you need concentration, you need time. Not time to decide whether to hit or stand... of course not. That's second nature to me. And it should become that way to you, too. Counters need time to see all the cards and compute the values. And, frankly, they need time to relax, even for a fleeting moment, during play.

The argument that a faster game speed will only result in more winnings for a card-counter is sheer foolishness. You've already learned that the great majority of playing time is not in the black, but in the red. Maybe not blood red, but certainly not better than a break-even. The game has a negative expectation most of the time, so what's the point of rushing the inevitable?

I remember one counter telling me recently that he only wants to play at a table with a few, if any, other players. He must have the speed. He says he wants to be able to play more than one spot when the cards are favorable. Although there is some merit to his reasoning, **I personally prefer to play at a *full* table today, at the last player position (third base) so I can see as many cards as possible before I have to act on my hand.** I'll give up the advantage of playing multiple spots in order to see more cards.

Blackjack players today, thinking that they are so good, figure that the more hands they play, the more they win. No. The game may be good. But it's not *that* good. Even if *you* are.

As I completed my writing about this important aspect of blackjack, I tried to recall a story from all my years of play that would help you understand the dramatic impact that game speed can have on your gaming record. I believe in taking many breaks when I gamble, so I was all prepared to tell you how to go about doing this by telling you a story about a player who doesn't believe in breaks. He plays in marathon sessions. I'm sure that's all the information you need to write your own ending. I'm also sure you can understand how taking breaks can cut down on decisions. Personally, I couldn't play without an agenda of decisive breaks from the action. But a story like this seemed too patronizing. I was stumped for a way to really convince you exactly how important this issue is.

And then the phone call came in.

It was one of my best craps-playing buddies, Marvin Karlins, who told me he just got back from a gambling excursion on a cruise ship and wanted to tell me all about it. Gamblers do that. We all like to talk about our gambling experiences. We're worse than a bunch of old ladies at a church social. But Marvin's stories are always better than most. He's a good storyteller, which is probably why he's a bestselling novelist. (In case you're not a fiction-freak, you can read Karlins' gambling wisdoms in *The Book Casino Managers Fear The Most.*) Although his experience he was about to tell me was at a dice table, it fits in perfectly for this piece. Read on. It doesn't make any difference if you know the game or not.

Marvin had been playing for a few hours, and was winning... and tipping the dealers as Marvin likes to do whenever the dealers are super-nice to the players. But dealers like Marvin not just for his tips, but because he's fun to be around. He can bring excitement to a dull table in no time. Chalk up the first day at the tables as successful for Marvin, *and* for the dealers.

The next day, Marvin was ready for another crack at them. There was only one dice table so there wasn't much question where to play. Same table, same dealers, same boss. But this time, it wasn't so much fun as before. The dealers were rushing the players for their bets, and the stickman was rushing the dice to the shooter before all the bets were made! The dice would almost always hit a player's hand as bets were made late. What a commotion!

The clincher came when Marvin told me about the dice flying off the table. The shooter said, "Same dice," which means exactly what it sounds like. A shooter always has this privilege. If he wants the same dice, a boss has to scurry around to find the die on the floor, check it out, and return it to the table. It takes time, but, as I said, it's a standard rule that all casinos go along with.

But not on this ship they don't. Not anymore. As soon as the shooter requested the same die that bounced off the table, the stickman emptied the bowl of extra dice and pushed them to the shooter. "Not this time, buddy. Pick two and shoot 'em!"

Marvin became frustrated. He quit the table early and found the casino manager to complain about the way the game was being run. How could the dealers be so friendly one day and so pushy the next?

"The word just came down," said the casino manager.

"Word? What word?" said Marvin, thinking to himself that if "the word just came down," it must have come from up on high because the casino and the executive offices were on the top level of the ship! If any word came down, it must have come from the crow's nest!

"Yep, we got the word all right," says the casino boss. "Management wants more decisions. Here's the E-Mail. You want to read it? If they want more decisions, we need to play this game faster. We only have one dice table!"

Translation: Management wants to make more money! And it's all because of the F-word. No, not friendly... financial. Or maybe it should be the C-word: Corporate.

Oh, happy day! In the middle of Marvin's joyride through the Caribbean, the cruise ship's management decides to push the throttles. And a lot of players got caught in the wake.

The moral to his story is easy, isn't it? If more decisions are good for the casino, do you think they are good for you?

Optimum Strategy

There's no question how to bet blackjack. Like craps, there's only one preferred way: In its most simplistic definition, you bet more when you have an edge; bet less when you don't.

Since we've already covered the details of basic strategy and card-counting in Chapter 5, you know exactly what to do: Simply follow basic strategy for all of your player options, and learn either of the two card-counting strategies I showed you. That's it. Simple, isn't it? Well, it is and it isn't, because most players won't take the time to master basic strategy (let's hope they at least keep the strategy cards handy), and they won't bother with card-counting at all. For those of you I've just described, here's the next best thing to do:

A Counting Overview

I introduced this concept in 1982, and later revised it in the first edition of *Casino Games* in 1985. Yeah, I know... it seems like ancient history. What really scares me is that some readers might not have even been born in 1982! But it worked then and works just as well today. Let me tell you about it.

The real significance of card-counting turns up, with no surprise, when the count is running at the extremes. If I may borrow the terms that Woody and I used, I'm talking about the times when the cards are black as midnight, or red as blood. That's when the decisions on altering basic strategy and adjusting your bets (called bet-sizing) are the most pronounced.

I've also found that most players who understand card-counting, but don't necessarily practice it, seem to know when these extremes are reached just by keeping a watch of the cards. No fancy memorizing. No counting up and down. No plus this or minus that.

When the remaining cards are rich in 10s and aces, these "observers" of the cards seem to know it as well as an actual counter. They know it by watching for either the little cards or the big ones. Not both. Too much to do, I guess. Most players who go this route choose to count just the little cards. This practice is what I call a "half-count."

Although it's not as accurate as counting both little cards and big ones, it does work because one group is usually relative to the other. When an excess of little cards are out of the shoe, you suspect there's an excess of aces and 10s remaining. And the reverse is usually true: If you don't see an excess of little cards, then you can pretty much guess they're still in the shoe. What you don't know, and will never know, is which side of the cut-card they're on.

Counting both the little cards and the big cards serves to really tweak your number. It's more accurate. It's the way I hope you choose to go. But if you decide to just do a counting overview, you might be interested in hearing that the results are remarkably similar... most of the time.

Can you at least do that? Can you at least do a cursory count of just the little cards? You can? But you wonder why I spent all those pages teaching you two full-blown plus/minus count strategies if doing this "half-count" is almost as good.

Well, maybe I need to tell you why it's not as accurate. Go up three paragraphs and catch the sentence: "When an excess of little cards are out of the shoe, you suspect there's an excess of aces and 10s remaining." But how do you know that the little cards that have escaped the shoe represent an excessive amount for that point in the shoe?

Maybe the little cards just seem like a lot but are really no more or less than the norm at that particular point. Do you see? By counting both little cards and big ones, you know whether or not the ratio is off kilter. By just counting one side, you have to make an educated guess. And let me help you with that one, too. It helps to know that for every 13 cards you see, five cards should be little (2, 3, 4, 5, or 6). If you see significantly more, bet a little more. If you see significantly less, bet a little less.

The Ace Count

It's a stretch to call this a count strategy, but it beats no strategy at all. It's the easiest of all of them: Simply keep track of the aces. It's the only card worth counting if you're only going to count one!

Know how many decks you're playing against. Multiple that number by four and you've got the total for the shoe. Grade school math.

Let's say you're playing at a table with an eight-deck shoe. There are 32 aces, all of which you would like to see land in front of you. But regardless of where they land, count 'em. If you're half way through the shoe, you should have seen 16. A quarter of the way through, eight should have appeared. Got it? Remember, bet accordingly. But don't take this count to the bank. Let it be only a general guide in your bet-sizing.

The Four-Color Strategy
For Blackjack

For those of you who only want to play basic strategy, there's no reason why you can't apply the Four-Color Strategy to this great game. There are streaks at blackjack, although not as frequently as at the dice tables. Considering a hand of black-jack as a nearly even bet (with basic strategy, it nearly is), you should experience streaks of eight to ten same decisions (win or lose) inside every run of 200 hands. Hopefully, these will be *win* decisions for you, but don't be so naive as to think you can't lose ten hands in a row. If you can win ten in a row, you can lose ten in a row. But I would like to think that all the discussions we had in Chapter 2 about Four-Color betting will prevent a losing streak from mounting to such an extreme. Follow the exit rules, as I do, regardless of which strategy, if any, you're playing.

If you jumped to the blackjack chapters without reading Chapters 1 and 2, go back and do it now. **The Four-Color Strategy is based on my favorite gambler's maxim: Let the winnings run; lay back or quit when you're losing.**

Double Double

I really can't end this chapter without mentioning an off-beat betting strategy that I play, especially at the blackjack tables... and roulette, too, if I'm so inclined. It has no mathematical basis behind it. In fact, it has no basis at all, except one: I've played it for so long, so successfully, that I really can't remember a time when I *didn't* play it.

It's based on a run of three wins with two presses. Let's say we start with $5. If I win it, I press it to $10. If that bet wins, the whole $20 goes. If it wins, *I* go! With a tidy $35 profit.

There actually is a reason behind my success with the Double Double, at least there is at the blackjack tables. I'm always counting, as you might imagine. And I only play it when my count is strong.

When I first started experimenting with this bet, my son was only about three or four years old. He picked up on the name and would always ask me when I called home how my "Gobble Gobble" was doing. Maybe that's a better name for it. After all, the idea is to gobble money from the casino!

The bet, over all these years, has made me just a bit too popular in some casinos. Winning does tend to call attention to yourself. But the bet spread is only two. It should tickle no one's interest... unless I start with a quarter and walk with one-seventy-five. Still, there are blackjack dealers who know me only because of this goofy bet. And I have to believe it's because I win it so often.

Some things you just don't argue with.

Summary

Blackjack is a game that most new players hear about in terms associated with its hey-day of years ago. It was a time when there were more blackjack players than slot players, if you can believe that today.

Of all the reasons I've cited why this "beatable" game is not so beatable anymore, I urge you to recall the discussion about casino countermeasures. I touched upon this briefly in the previous chapter but it's worth repeating. Casino countermeasures have nothing to do with the way players play, but everything to do with the way *casinos* play the game.

The game has been toughened since the good ol' days. It's important that you know that. If you want a good read on this subject, try John Alcamo's

Casino Gambling Behind The Tables. I've always recommended this book to players who start thinking about playing professionally. But it's not just about blackjack; it's about all the games. John spills a lot of privy information. In the world of casino gambling, knowledge is power.

So what goes at the top of your ever-growing compendium of knowledge? That's right. You'll read it five times in *Budget Gambling:*

If you can't afford to lose it, don't bet it.

CHAPTER 7

Roulette:
Rules Of The Game

By now, I'm sure you've realized that I like to tell you about the games in a rather informal style. It's as if I'm sitting with you in your living room and we're just having a casual conversation. Think back to your college days and I'm sure you'll agree that "casual" wins over "formal" in the learning process. Most students prefer smaller classes with an open-forum relationship with their teacher. Got a question? Ask it. It certainly beats an auditorium full of students taking notes from a lecture they can barely hear, from a teacher they can barely see. One might as well watch a TV monitor.

Well, we really can't have a conversation, and you really can't ask questions, but I would like you to know that this manuscript was presented to a host of beginner players before publication, to garner queries. When questions were raised, the answers were rewritten into the manuscript. Guess which chapter earned the most questions. That's right. This one.

Why not blackjack with all the complexities of card-counting? Probably because players today are becoming more suspicious of the game, and are no longer taking the serious approach to it that was common in years past. Why not craps? Probably because it turned out to be far less complicated than these players imagined. But why roulette? Well, since most of the questions fell within the same category, maybe it shouldn't have surprised me.

Most often, players wanted to know more about betting systems (I prefer the term *strategy*). You see, roulette is the game of systems. For hundreds of years, roulette enthusiasts have tried to crack this game with system after system. You've probably heard some of the stories. Some of the greatest mathematicians have put their minds to the test, knowing full well there were more important things to study, but the roulette wheel was probably more fun.

There are documented stories of colossal wins at the roulette table, some even breaking the bank, and, of course, all accomplished through the means of a revolutionary system. A system so hush-hush that players would put their lives on the line to protect it. A system so powerful that a king would offer millions in jewels for the secret. A roulette system that worked was worth more than the secrets of life.

Today, nothing has changed. Newer high-tech systems have made the national media. Even leading software designers have risen to the challenge. That's right. All kinds of computer gadgetry are being used to beat the wheel. It leaves some casino managers wondering if they have to metal-test players before they sit down to play.

As long as the systems that players use don't have anything to do with gadgets, casino managers don't care. In fact, most casinos today post the previous winning numbers on a big electronic scoreboard right there at the table. Casinos encourage players to invent systems based on the prior numbers that have come up. Why do they encourage it? Because it encourages play. And that's all the casino wants... players playing. The game has a solid advantage for the house, so the more players play, the more the house wins. It's no different from a retail store putting up signs in the window to lure customers.

But what you should realize from this tactic is an obvious one: If the casino management has no qualms about displaying all the previous winning numbers, do you think it could possibly help you to know what these numbers are?

I don't think so. **The casino is never going to do anything that will help you win.** If you owned the casino, would *you*? All the scoreboard really does, as I said, is promote more play. It can only give gullible players a false sense of advantage.

What the casino knows—and what you are about to learn—is that all the previous results have absolutely no bearing on future results. Let's say that a black number wins three times in a row. Do you think there's any mechanical or even mystical influence on the wheel to produce a red number just because black has won three times in a row? Think about it. It's a screwy notion, isn't it? But it's the basis of many a player's cockeyed strategy. A strategy that can only lead you where the casino wants you to go: into your pocket for more money.

Any beginner knows the basics of this game: Just guess where the little white ball is going to land. You can make even-money bets like red or black, or a slew of other bets that pay anywhere from 2 to 1 for a 12-number bet to 35 to 1 for a single number. And that's the bet most players like. That's right. Let's put the whole shebang on 29 black. Hey, there are only 38 compartments. You have a 1 in 38 chance of winning. These are not death-defying odds. We're not talking a 1 in 10,000,000 chance of lining up four 7s on a slot machine. Now that, my friend, is a leap of faith.

And the wheel is such a simple, mechanical thing. It hasn't changed in 200 years. We're not talking black-box here. There are no microprocessors inside the wheel like a slot machine has; there's nothing to distrust. Oh, go ahead, look under the table. You won't find any magnets, either.

There has to be a way to beat this thing. All gamblers who have ever met the wheel would be lying if they told you they never thought about it. It's just that some gamblers have taken their cause to a greater height with a space-age war cry: If we can put a man on the moon...

Roulette Rally

For the next few pages, I'm going to show you the many different bets that you can make at roulette, and go over the do's and don'ts that you must follow. There aren't many. But as we go along, I'm sure you'll be thinking about our discussion on systems, wondering if there really is a betting system that might work, and, after all these years, whether or not the roulette wheel has finally met its match in the computer age.

And it's good that you do. Because without the idea of system-play, without the mental challenge of the wheel's apparent invincibility, this game is a yawner.

Even though roulette is the casino's signature game, it just isn't getting the play that it used to. Most of the blame has been put on its relatively high percentage—a little over five percent—but that really isn't the culprit.

To put it bluntly, younger players are plain bored with it. And for that I feel sorry. No. Not for the players, but for the game itself. Roulette is the patriarch of all games of chance. It has survived the ages. But in today's fast-paced world of casino gambling, it is an endangered species.

The Basics

The most important distinction to note as you walk up to the table is that roulette is played with special chips. Each player has his or her own color. And that particular color has a particular value. If you would like yellow chips, and you would like each chip to be worth $1, simply give the dealer a twenty-dollar bill, and you'll receive 20 yellow chips. If you would like each chip to be worth $5, 20 chips will cost you $100.

Even though casinos today like to handle roulette chips in stacks of 20, you certainly don't have to buy the chips in multiples of 20, nor do you have to buy 20 chips at all. But it seems to have become the standard for most seasoned roulette players. Keeping the chips in stacks of 20 does aid basic accounting and makes payoffs easier.

Roulette chips have a value only at the roulette table and only at that particular table where you bought them. Never leave the table with roulette chips in your pocket. You might be stuck if you do. Remember, always cash in before you leave.

If no other player is using regular casino chips, the dealer will probably let you use them. Before I play, I always check to see if any players are already using them. If not, I do. I rarely play with roulette chips. And there's a reason:

When it's time for me to quit, I want to retreat the same way I leave any other table-game: Quickly. No temptations for another bet. No standing around. I take my chips and I'm gone. But if I'm using roulette chips, I must wait for the dealer to clear the table of losing bets, pay any winners, eventually catch my attention, take my chips, cut them out in stacks of 20, confirm the chip value, and then pay me (in regular casino chips).

Nope. That's not for me. Because I follow my Four-Color rules religiously, I also must go to the cage after each session to get my chips cashed into *real* cash. It's the only time in a casino when I'm in a hurry: when I'm leaving.

There are chairs around the table. Most players use them. Some don't. For various reasons (one very important one we'll learn about later), there are players who prefer to stand, even if it means standing behind seated players. Which means one has to lean over these players to make one's wager. Which can mean spilling a player's drink, knocking over their neatly stacked chips (stacks of 20, of course), messing up their coiffure (oh, excuse me, lady), well you get the idea. My advice to first-time players is to sit, even if it means away from the wheel, or away from your favorite section of the layout. The fact is, the layout is long. There is always a certain amount of leaning to do. The best seat, as you might guess, is at the center of the layout.

The wheel most often found in American casinos has 38 numbered compartments: the numbers 1 through 36 plus 0 and 00. Eighteen of the numbers are black and 18 of the numbers are red. The numbers 0 and 00 are green. The wheel is laid out so that the red and black numbers alternate, except near the green numbers. Virtually all table designs today position the wheel at the far end of the table. Players don't actually sit around the wheel; they sit around the betting layout, which I'll go over in detail later on.

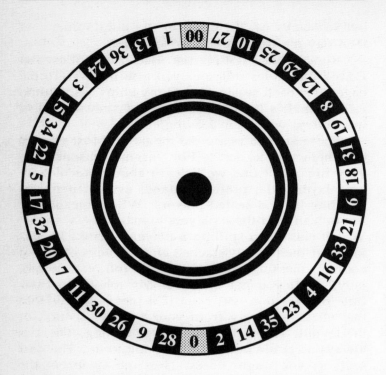

There are eleven different kinds of bets that you can make: a single number, groups of two, three, four, five, six, or twelve numbers; a column of twelve numbers, whether the number is red or black, odd or even, little or big (from 1 to 18 or 19 to 36). I'll discuss each of these bets at the end of this chapter. But, for now, let's get on with it. You've got your seat, you've got your chips. But before we bet, let's just watch for a moment.

To start each game, a dealer propels a white ball around a track at the upper level of the wheel's housing. The great suspense of this game is, of course, watching the little white ball slowly diminish in speed, drop from its track, bounce against deflectors (called "canoes" because they are shaped like one), drop down into the bowl of the wheel, bounce several more times as it hits the ridges of the compartments (called "frets," just like the little ridges on your guitar), and, after all this bouncing around, land in a compartment where it will stay, unless the dealer pushes a button that activates an electro-magnet, which will make it jump out and into another compartment.

Don't take me seriously.

The dealer announces the winning number and places a clear plastic marker on that number on the layout. All the bets that didn't win are quickly scooped away by the dealer, leaving only those bets that are awaiting a payoff. You might notice that several different-colored chips were placed on that winning number, all now sitting under the marker. It simply means that several players placed a bet on the same number. Some numbers might get so hot that a tall stack of different-colored chips (called a barber pole) leans precariously on the layout.

It's important that you do not place any new bets during the time the dealer is paying off winning bets. You must not make any new bets until the dealer has announced, "Place your bets."

It's also important that you do not watch the little white ball spin around the big wooden wheel. Oh, you've already done that? Feeling a little dizzy, huh? The ball spins one direction, the wheel spins the other. You've heard of car sickness or airplane sickness? Well, there's also roulette sickness. If you must watch the wheel, you'll need to take two Dramamine about an hour before you play. Oh, and call me in the morning.

The rule on making bets is a bit loose with some casinos, and more stringent at others. Generally, you are not allowed to bet after the dealer has called, "No more bets," supposedly at about the time when the ball is about to drop from its track.

Inside Outside

Now it's time to actually make a bet or two, assuming you're feeling better... and that Scotch on the rocks really did help you. If the whole casino has stopped spinning around in your head, let's give it a shot.

The table layout is your road map to fun and fortune. Look it over and you'll see that all the bets can be divided into two types: inside and outside.

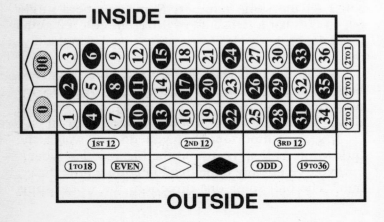

Inside bets: This section of the layout gets the most action. Most of the bets offer higher payoffs in line with the longer odds of winning. You can make a:

- one-number bet and win 35 times your wager.
- two-number bet and win 17 times your wager.
- three-number bet and win 11 times your wager.
- four-number bet and win 8 times your wager.
- six-number bet and win 5 times your wager.

A five-number bet is offered but not recommended.

Outside bets: This section of the layout is for the more conservative bets, in the sense that the bets are either even-money (if you bet a dollar, you win a dollar) or short-odds propositions. **For players with a small stake, the outside bets are the wiser choice because they have a more realistic chance of winning in the short term.** The even-money wagers are: red or black, odd or even, and big or little (from 1 to 18 or 19 to 36). The other outside wagers are merely two different ways to bet 12 numbers, both paying off at two times your wager.

Betting Limits

Roulette fits the requirements for *Budget Gambling* in the sense that the house usually sets relatively low minimums. The table might be a $5 minimum, but you don't have to make each bet $5. Generally speaking, the casino will allow you to spread the $5 over several bets, such as five bets at $1 each. Most casinos, however, will only

allow you to do this within either the inside or
outside sections. Think of it as a $5 minimum for
the inside bets and a $5 minimum for the outside
bets. *Always ask before you play so that you know
the betting rules at that particular casino.*

Surprisingly, most casinos set a relatively small
maximum betting limit for inside wagers. At a $5
table, it's not unusual to find betting limits of $100,
for example. The casino's reasoning on this
restricted maximum-bet limit is based on the high
payoffs for inside betting. With higher maximum-
bet limits typical of other table-games, smaller
casinos could be hurt by a roulette player on an
incredible win streak.

I've always wondered about the casino's apparent fear of inside bettors, as evidenced by this
greatly reduced maximum-bet level. Do you suppose it might be because casinos are not that
convinced that a roulette wheel can produce purely
random, unpredictable numbers? It's the subject of
the next chapter. But first things first. Here's a
page-by-page detail of making all the wagers:

STRAIGHT-UP BET (One Number)

A straight-up bet is simply a bet on a single number. On our sample layout, I've shown a straight-up bet on the numbers 14, 29, and 0. Since there are 38 different compartments on the wheel, there are 38 different straight-up bets you can make. You can wager on as many different numbers as you like.

Be sure you place your chip completely inside the boxed number. Don't touch a line, because that will denote a different type of bet that I'll cover next.

A straight-up bet pays 35 to 1.

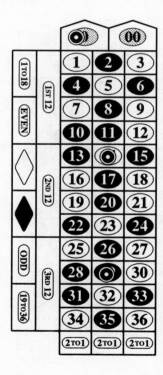

SPLIT BET (Two Numbers)

A split bet is made by placing your chip on the line that separates two adjacent numbers on the layout.

A split bet gives you two numbers that are working for you on the next spin of the wheel. If either number hits, you win!

On our illustration, I've indicated three split bets: the numbers 4 and 5; 16 and 19; and 0 and 1.

There are 62 different ways to make a split bet.

A split bet pays 17 to 1.

STREET BET (Three Numbers)

A street bet gives you three numbers with just one wager. The bet is made by placing your chip as shown on our layout, on the line that separates the inside and outside betting area, giving you that particular row of three numbers (a street). I've shown the street numbers 7, 8, and 9 placed. In addition, you can make a street bet on the 1, 0, and 2; the 2, 0, and 00 (as shown); and on the 2, 00, and 3.

There are 15 possible combinations of three-number wagers you can make.

A street bet pays 11 to 1.

CORNER BET (Four Numbers)

A corner bet is one of the most popular bets at the roulette table, but don't ask me why.

The chip must be placed at the junction of four numbers. I've indicated two different four-number bets on the layout: 20, 21, 23, and 24; and 1, 2, 4, and 5.

There are 22 possible corner bets that you can make.

A corner bet pays 8 to 1.

FIVE-NUMBER BET (Five Numbers)

This bet is the only one that is not recommended, because the house advantage is greater than the game's otherwise consistent 5.26 percent.

There's no particular reason to make this bet, and every reason not to. So, let's not spend much time on it. Forget it.

The five-number bet pays 6 to 1.

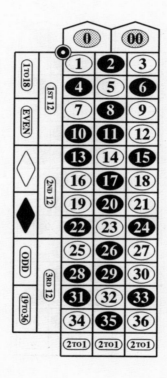

LINE BET (Six Numbers)

Here's a relatively unpopular bet that provides you with six numbers for a single wager. Think of it as a double street bet where you have two adjacent streets of numbers.

This bet must be placed between two rows of three numbers, on the line at the left of the inside layout.

There are 11 ways to make a six-number bet.

The line bet pays 5 to 1.

COLUMN BET (Twelve Numbers)

The column bet is an outside wager that allows you to cover 12 numbers, representing one of the three vertical columns of numbers.

On the sample illustration, I've bet the column at the far right, beginning with 3 and ending with 36. Most column players prefer this row because the numbers in the column are easy to remember: the common multiples of 3 (3, 6, 9, 12, 15 and so on).

There are obviously three different ways to make a column bet. **Column bets pay 2 to 1 odds.**

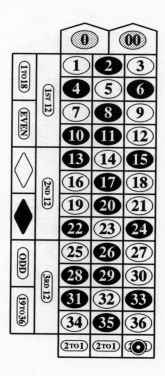

DOZEN BET (Twelve Numbers)

This bet is another way of covering 12 numbers, but unlike the column bet, the numbers are in numerical order: 1 through 12, 13 through 24, and 25 through 36.

Your wager should be placed in the outside section indicating the first 12, second 12, or third 12. The dozen bet represents another popular wager.

On the sample layout, I've indicated a dozen bet for the middle third, 13 through 24.

The dozen bet pays 2 to 1.

RED OR BLACK (18 Numbers)

This is the bet that most novice players like to make. You have the best likelihood of winning as compared to the inside wagers, but the payout is greatly reduced to even money. Not surprisingly, the largest wagers at a roulette table are made on "red or black."

The diamonds at the far left center of the betting layout are in black and red, and indicate the position for making this wager.

A red or black bet pays 1 to 1 odds.

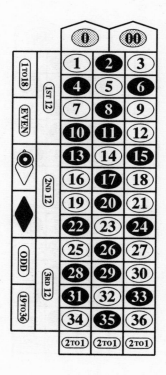

ODD OR EVEN (18 Numbers)

This bet is similar to the red or black wager I just described, except you're betting on whether the number that wins is an odd or even number. Like red or black, you have only two choices. It can't be that tough.

The boxes for making this bet are easily identified.

An odd or even bet pays 1 to 1 odds.

1-18 OR 19-36 BET (18 Numbers)

This bet is another even-money proposition, whereby you're guessing whether the winning number is low or high.
Again, the correct box for making the wager is obvious.
Of the three even-money wagers, this bet is the least popular.
The 1-18 or 19-36 bet pays 1 to 1 odds.

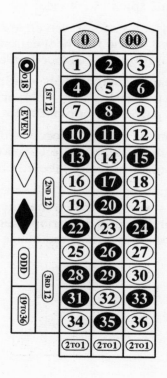

Neat Things To Know

- A pair of even numbers alternates with a pair of odd numbers, except when adjacent to the green numbers.

- Odd numbers are directly opposite the next highest even number.

- The wheel spins in a counterclockwise direction; the ball spins clockwise.

- What seems like motor-driven motion is actually achieved by the flywheel action of the heavy wheel (over 100 lbs.) balanced on a centerpoint.

- Casinos change their wheels routinely to guard against the possibility that a player might detect a bias in a particular compartment or segment.

- Numbers on the roulette scoreboard are recorded automatically by a photo-cell sensor that detects the ball in electronically labeled compartments.

- In illegal gaming houses of the past, some roulette dealers were so skilled that they could make the ball land within a certain segment of the wheel... a section where the house had the fewest wagers.

CHAPTER 8

Roulette:
Budget Gambling
Strategies

Before we get into some really heavy-duty strategies to give that darn wheel a workout, let's talk about zeros. Green zeros. In the last chapter, I casually mentioned that most American casinos use a wheel with 38 numbered compartments made up of 18 red numbers, 18 black numbers, and two green numbers. Those green numbers are 0 and 00. From here on out, let's refer to the zeros as a "single zero" and a "double zero." When I refer to a double-zero wheel, it means the wheel has both the single zero and double zero.

All bets at a double-zero wheel, with the exception of the five-number bet, earn a hefty percentage for the house of 5.26 percent. That's *every* bet, mind you... whether you're betting red or black or some long-odds inside bet. Every time you whiz through a hundred-dollar bill, you're forking over five dollars and 26 cents... over the long term, of course.

And what can we blame for that nasty percentage against us? Why the green numbers, of course. If it were not for the two green spots on the wheel, the game would be a toss-up. The house wouldn't make a penny. But we wouldn't, either. Though we'd gladly take it, right? Just think of it! Free entertainment! Yeah, I know, you'd rather have that 5.26 percent on *your* side. Well, to do that, you'll have to run your own wheel in your basement. Put up your sign: Bob's Casino, downstairs.

Since that idea won't work, and the casino isn't about to take those two green spots off the wheel, maybe we can talk them into taking *one* of the spots off. Shop around and you might find one. It's called a "single zero" wheel and... that's right, it only has 37 compartments. What's really nice is that the payoffs are the same as a double-zero wheel. You thought that was how they were going to make up for it, huh? Stiff you with smaller payoffs? Nope. Same payoffs, and you've got one less number to worry about.

Since the single-zero wheel pays off at the same odds as the double-zero wheel, the house percentage is effectively reduced to 2.70 percent!

Several casinos, especially in Nevada and Atlantic City, have installed the more player-friendly European single-zero wheel in the hope of attracting more players. If you can't find one here, there's always Europe. If you're a frequent player, the money you save will probably cover your airfare.

But wait! There's more! You'll also find another player advantage over there called "en prison." This popular feature means that if the ball lands on zero, there is no decision on any of the even-money wagers that would have otherwise been lost. The bets are placed "in prison" until the next spin of the wheel. Then, if the bets win, they are only "removed from prison" (not paid). It's then up to the players to either make their bets again, or remove them from the table. The net effect of "en prison" is that the house edge is cut even further to 1.35 percent! Wow! The Europeans really know how to run a casino!

Here in the good ol' U.S. of A., you might find a similar feature called "surrender." So far, anyhow, the only reports I've heard of casinos using surrender have been at a double-zero wheel. *Surrender* means that if you are betting on any of the even-money wagers, the dealer will only remove one-half of your bet if the ball lands in a green compartment. Surrender at a double-zero wheel effectively cuts the house edge to 2.63 percent.

Incidentally, a player recently wrote to tell me that she had found several single-zero wheels while vacationing in Northern Nevada. She was elated until she found out that all the single-zero wheels had a $25 minimum bet posted! Why does that not surprise me?

Here's a chart that lists all of the bets, and gives the percentages in consideration of single-zero and double-zero wheels, surrender, and "en prison."

ROULETTE PAYTABLES			DOUBLE ZERO		SINGLE ZERO	
TYPE OF WAGER	NUMBERS COVERED	ACTUAL PAYOFF	CORRECT ODDS	HOUSE EDGE	CORRECT ODDS	HOUSE EDGE
Straight-Up	1	35:1	37:1	5.26	36:1	2.70
Split	2	17:1	18:1	5.26	17.5:1	2.70
Street	3	11:1	11.7:1	5.26	11.3:1	2.70
Corner	4	8:1	8.5:1	5.26	8.25:1	2.70
Five-Number	5	6:1	6.6:1	7.89	Not Available	
Line	6	5:1	5.3:1	5.26	5.17:1	2.70
Column	12	2:1	2.2:1	5.26	2.1:1	2.70
Dozen	12	2:1	2.2:1	5.26	2.1:1	2.70
Red/Black	18	1:1	1.1:1 (1.05:1)	5.26 (2.63)	1.05:1 (1.03:1)	2.70 (1.35)
Odd/Even	18	1:1	1.1:1 (1.05:1)	5.26 (2.63)	1.05:1 (1.03:1)	2.70 (1.35)
1-18/19-36	18	1:1	1.1:1 (1.05:1)	5.26 (2.63)	1.05:1 (1.03:1)	2.70 (1.35)

The numbers in parentheses are the odds and percentages for either "surrender" or "en prison" that some casinos permit on the even-money wagers.

Optimum Betting

It's difficult to provide a betting strategy for roulette that would suggest it is the best of all the others. This game is so mathematically locked up for the house that it is probably the best example of a negative-expectation game. You should also know that any betting strategy cannot change a negative-expectation game into a positive-expectation game... at least, not in the long term. But, if you recall from our opening chapter, an important component of *Budget Gambling* is minimizing exposure. Difficult as it may be, try to keep your play within the short term, because it is in short-term play that betting strategies can prove valuable.

So, in that regard, my optimum strategy is really more of a set of recommendations:

1. Try to find a single-zero wheel with a low minimum-bet requirement.

2. Look for the "surrender" or "en prison" feature.

2. Make only even-money bets, such as red/black or odd/even.

3. Follow the Four-Color Strategy to the letter.

4. Reduce your number of sessions by taking longer breaks between them.

5. Play only at a full table. The more players, the less frequent the decisions. You'll probably have more fun at a crowded table, anyhow.

Parlay Party

If I were a lawyer, I would start this sub-heading with that classic legalese: "notwithstanding the foregoing." But I'm not a lawyer, thank you, so I'll simply say that "in spite of what I just told you," there is a neat little betting strategy that I would like to let you in on, one that does not exactly follow all my rules for optimum betting.

It doesn't take a beginner long to learn that the optimum way to gamble is rarely the fun way. It's that ominous fact that reminds me of this strategy that I call the "parlay party." A fitting term because what I remember best about it is the fun the players were having. So let me give you all the details.

I picked it up many years ago from friends who would drive to Vegas from San Bernadino, a mere four hour's drive. They were husband and wife, her sister and boyfriend. And all they played was roulette. And all they had was fun!

It was such an experience for them that they would actually dress for the occasion. I mean *formal* dress: suit and tie, evening gowns... in a term borrowed from that era, they were dressed to the nines.

This fearsome foursome would commandeer a wheel and settle in for the night. In fact, evenings were the only time they played. A nice dinner, then the fun begins. And sometimes the fun would run well into the night. Not to mention the runs of luck. It was incredible at times, and I was witness to many a session.

No even-money wagers for this team as you might have guessed, and no long-shot single-number bets, either. All they played were "dozen" bets: the three outside sections of numbers that represented the first, second, and third groups of twelve. You know, 1 through 12, 13 through 24, and 25 through 36. The only numbers they couldn't bet— the only numbers that didn't fit into the dozens— were those dastardly green zeros.

They only had two basic rules to remember: (1) Follow the wheel, and (2) win two in a row. What made their strategy work so well was the 2 to 1 payoff. You see, the essence of the strategy was to win a bet, parlay it, and win the second. A $5 bet would yield a tidy profit of $40! Whether they won the bet following a win or not, the next bet would always revert back to the nickel. It was a nickel-and-dime betting scheme that would generate sizeable profits when it worked. And when it didn't work, the losses were minimal.

By using the term *follow the wheel,* I mean mimicking the previous result. It has no real basis of fact, of course, but that's the way they played. They let the wheel tell them what to bet. If a number in the first dozen hit, the next bet would be the first dozen again, and again, until it lost. If the bet lost because a third-dozen number hit, for example, the next bet would be the third dozen.

Obviously, they were hoping for streaks. And I have no quarrel with that, either. Regardless of the game I play, I always play for streaks, too. Whether streaks of numbers, or streaks of wins, riding a streak with progressive betting is the hallmark of *Budget Gambling.*

Let's look at their strategy in a little more detail. Since the second bet following a win is a full press of the initial bet *and the winnings,* this is a true parlay wager. If you lose either of the two bets, you lose the nickel. If you win both bets, you win $40. Simple. Effective. And, in the realm of today's million-to-one odds at the slot machines, bucking 8 to 1 odds at the roulette table is certainly "in the realm."

I doubt that my friends of long ago really knew, or cared, about the odds of winning two in a row. With the game percentage figured in, it's a little steeper than 8 to 1, but if they didn't care, why should we? Like I said, the object of their little game was to string two wins together. That's all. That's all they cared about. Beat the wheel in the short term. That's all. That's all they cared about.

Throw a few wins together, and that opening bet of a nickel grew to a dime. A few more wins and the dime grew to a quarter. Now you can see how on a very successful night, they would all go up to their rooms and sleep like a baby. There was no competition among them, no jealousy, because they all played the same bets. They all won the same, or they all lost the same.

Allow me to expand on their strategy with an interesting chart that shows the power of a parlay with a 2 to 1 payoff:

BET	WIN	COLLECT	NET WIN
$ 5	$ 10	$ 15	$ 10
15	30	45	40
45	90	135	130
135	270	405	400

I'm not suggesting that you modify the "win two" rule and go for a run of four. That's 80 to 1 odds, throw in the house percentage, and forget it. But it is interesting to look at, and that's all we should do with it. Unless, of course, you want to risk that nickel that you just built into 130 smackers, because you want to take it "one more time." Well, "one more time" is usually the proverbial "kiss," so let me present a variation on my friends' strategy that's only a quasi-parlay. That is, we'll only "parlay" the even-money winnings and keep the odds payoffs safely intact.

BET	WIN	COLLECT	KEEP	NET WIN
$ 5	$10	$ 15	$ 5	$ 10
10	20	30	10	30
20	40	60	20	70
40	80	120	120	150

Unlike the parlay party of four, who tried to beat the wheel through guesswork, some fancy guesswork to be sure, a new wave of assault on the wheel sprang up during that decade, and it all had to do with "clocking the wheel."

I remember a pit boss at a downtown Vegas casino telling me that they let their customers "time" their wheels with stopwatches. "It's like a miniature derby down here," he said, "Everyone gathers around the wheel with a stopwatch around their neck."

There were at least three popular variations on the concept of wheel clocking, and they all had three things in common: Gauge the speed of the wheel relative to the speed of the ball, correlate the diminishing speed to an arbitrary number on the wheel, and then compare the winning number to the arbitrary number as a relational variant. With a little practice, it was thought, there could be some predictability as to a particular segment of the wheel where the ball might land.

As the wheel-clocking excitement gathered steam, some players would form teams of three, each member responsible for one of the three important bits of information to plug into this fascinating equation.

Well, I got into the act, too. But I took a different tact to solving the puzzle. Instead of clocking the wheel, I suggested clocking the dealer! The idea was sound, but the technology simply wasn't available to pull it off. At least not yet.

Clocking The Dealer

The essence of clocking a dealer is to determine if there is any pattern to the spot on the wheel where the ball is released, and the spot where the ball lands.

Roulette dealers show an uncanny and unintentional tendency to spin the ball at remarkably similar speeds, time and time again.

Since the dealers spin the ball so many times each day, week in and week out, they develop a programmed motion, much as we all try to do swinging a golf club or rolling a bowling ball. Their "delivery" becomes grooved, especially if they've been doing it for a long time. I concluded that there must be a relationship between the release-point and the drop-point of the ball if all other factors— namely, speeds—are relatively constant.

All a clocker would have to do is note the average location on the wheel where the ball drops and relate this area to the spot on the wheel where the dealer began the spin. Sounds simply enough. And it is, with a lot of practice... not to mention good eyesight. But how accurate is it? And what about the dealers? Wouldn't it seem likely that the dealers themselves would become aware of their novel ability?

If you're still not convinced that some experienced roulette dealers can develop a predictable routine, put yourself in their position. You've been working the wheel for years and years. After a while, isn't it likely that you would begin to wonder if you could skillfully control the outcome? Isn't it likely that you would eventually decide to "test" your skill during the course of your long workday? After all, you're being paid to spin the ball, so you might as well have some fun with it.

Surprisingly, a few dealers I talked to confirmed this notion. In fact, one dealer was quite bold in bragging about his "touch."

We can assume that no dealer can make the ball drop in a specific compartment, without some sort of trickery. That degree of legitimate skill would be virtually impossible, based on, at the very least, the many deflectors that guard the wheel and catch the ball. I didn't just fall off the onion truck, and neither did you.

And I'm not suggesting that any dealer has developed a skill to cheat you. In fact, I was told about a dealer who would occasionally feel sorry for a particular player and would try to help the player win! I'm not sure what it took to qualify for the "help," other than (a) you were losing badly, (b) you reminded him of his mother, or (c) you reminded him of Bo Derek.

I'm not a roulette dealer, so I can't tell you what goes through their minds, and I can't tell you, in fact, that a skill can be developed. Allowing plenty of room for exaggeration, who's to say that dealers with a lot of years under their belt can't provide at least a little influence? Who's to say that dealers have never fallen victim to their Good Samaritan values? And who's to say what might happen if you walk up to the table with a big cigar?

As you can appreciate, any dealer caught trying to help a player win (or lose), would be fired on the spot, although it would be difficult to prove. This brings to mind the possibility that some roulette dealers could indeed line their own pockets by working in collusion with players as their partners and splitting the profits.

There are stories about crooked roulette dealers in illegal joints of yesteryear who could make the ball drop in a section of the wheel where the house had no action or at least the smallest bets. If a big wager was made on 11, the ball would drop on the opposite side of the wheel. The dealer had the touch.

But the real point to this discussion should be obvious. If it's possible that certain experienced dealers can affect the outcome by their skill, doesn't that suggest that you could also develop a skill by measuring these same parameters?

Isn't it possible that at least some advantage can be gained, maybe 10 percent or even 20 percent effectiveness, in pinpointing a section of the wheel where the ball might drop?

If you notice that in eight out of ten times or so, the ball came to rest in a section of the wheel that's directly opposite the release area, that would certainly seem to indicate a possible pattern. Perhaps the ball came to rest near the same release area. That's fine. There's your section to use.

If you're concerned about the highly remote chance that some dealers will try to beat you with their skill, don't worry about it. Remember, you always place your bet after the ball has left the dealer's hand!

Which reminds me... try to make your bet as soon as possible. Don't push the limits to the point where the ball has already dropped. The dealer might think you're trying to past-post the game! The term *past-posting* means making a bet after the winning number has already been determined.

There are many snags that you should be aware of. For example, subtle variations in the wheel's speed (or the ball's speed) will make clocking totally useless. Although the dealer might be aware of these changes, you may have great difficulty in detecting them.

It's likely that if dealers suspect you're trying to clock them, they will purposely vary the speed of either the ball or the wheel to beat you at their own game. After all, the dealer has complete control over the parameters that you're trying to measure. Don't let them know that you're making the effort.

If you stand around a table for an hour or so with your nose two feet from the wheel, and make notes on a scratch pad while holding a chart of the wheel numbers, my guess is, it'll look a little fishy.

The slick wheel-clockers, whoever they are, are so professional that they can actually sit at the table (nearest to the wheel) and chat with the dealer and the players while doing incredible computations in their head. If they see a pattern after a few spins, they'll make several straight-up bets on numbers in a particular section, but not by looking at a chart of numbers. That's an obvious give-away. They have the numbers on the wheel memorized. And that's not easy!

If you're detected trying to clock the wheel, the floorperson will probably keep an eye on you. If you show that you're losing like everyone else, all you'll draw are a few chuckles. But if you're winning, whether your strategy is working or you're just plain lucky, you'll get some pressure. The floorperson will probably instruct the dealer to vary the speeds of the ball and the wheel, and to rush the time frame in which you can make your wagers.

At that stage, you might as well sit down, relax, and guess at the numbers like everyone else.

The High-Tech Strategy

Let me tell you how Keith and Margo play this
game.

Margo is stationed at the wheel. Keith is sitting
at the middle of the layout.

Margo's job is to signal Keith as to the section
of the wheel where the ball will most likely land.
Keith will then cover all the numbers in that particular section. How does Margo do it? I'll tell
you.

First of all, Margo wants everyone to think she's
a first-timer to the casino. She stands by the wheel,
mingling with casual on-lookers. It's important that
there are other people watching the wheel too, so
Margo can blend in.

Keith and Margo have coded each number on
the wheel with elaborate signs that would make
any baseball manager proud. Of course, there's no
need for her to do a Saint Vitus dance because
there's no one to steal the signals. One very subtle
signal... just for Keith.

Keith and Margo are recent college grads. Keith
is an electronics engineer. Margo is a software designer.

Margo can only predict the point on the wheel
where the ball will leave its track. She cannot pinpoint the number where the ball will land, but she
can identify the quadrant (a quarter of the wheel)
with an accuracy of 58 percent.

How does Margo do it? I'll tell you.

Margo knew there was a relationship between the point on the wheel where the dealer lets go of the ball, the diminishing speed of the ball, the diminishing speed of the wheel, and the point where the ball descends. All Margo had to do was design the computer software, plug in these four variables, and voilá! The ball will fall at 23. Not *in* 23, but it will leave its orbit at 23.

Keith studied roulette wheels with the same fervor that Margo had done. They made a great team. The biggest obstacles standing in the way of this team's success were the canoes (deflectors) positioned around the wheel.

There are eight canoes in alternating positions: One is positioned at a right angle to the wheel's circumference, the next one is parallel, and so on. Keith had determined that the right-angle canoes would actually "kick" the ball backward by up to four compartments over 40 percent of the time. Nearly 20 percent of the time, the ball would bounce over the canoe and roll forward by up to five compartments. The rest of the time, the ball would carom off a parallel canoe, catching the points, for example, in an unpredictable fashion.

How thankful he was that all the canoes were not parallel where only the points would come into play. But the right-angle canoes were square to the path of the dropping ball and made the deflection more predictable. In fact, Keith likes to say that the square canoes (as he called them) actually work against the concept of creating random numbers. The ball, he said, would most likely fall within nine compartments of that point where it hit the square canoe.

Indeed. Nearly 60 percent of the time, the ball would land in a compartment that was within a quadrant identified by the number Margo signaled and representing its center. They could guess at the quadrant and be accurate 25 percent of the time. A 58 percent accuracy meant they weren't guessing!

But how does Margo know the number? I'll tell you.

Keith designed a sensor to read two crossing speeds. The fact that the wheel spins counterclockwise and the ball spins clockwise made it easier to get the two readings. If both the ball and wheel were spinning in the same direction, it would have been nearly impossible to decipher the speeds. Here's another case where one of the game's design features (opposite-direction spinning) was thought to further the cause of unpredictability. But the result is that it *lends* predictability. Or, in this case, readability.

Keith built the sensor into the frames of Margo's glasses. Just above the nosepiece is the small lens that's camouflaged with decorative rhinestones. The sensor sends a signal to a computer in Margo's purse. The computer, in turn, sends an electronic signal to an output transducer that converts the electronic message into a series of clicks from a reed-relay fastened to the side of the purse. Margo feels the clicks and simply counts them to get her number.

All Margo really has to do to start the processing is tell the computer the location on the wheel where the dealer released the ball. Keith designed a clever key-pad system on the outside of her purse that looks like decorative brass buttons. She can feed in any of the 38 numbers by pressing only five buttons. The rest of the work is performed by the computer in a matter of seconds.

It makes no difference if the dealer slows down the wheel or changes the speed of the ball, because the computer's real-time analyzer is reading specific speeds for each game. There is no guesswork. Each game produces exacting data.

Keith, incidentally, has the entire wheel memorized. As soon as he gets the number from Margo, he places bets on that number, the four numbers above it, and the four numbers below it.

Bingo.

Players like Keith and Margo will continue to milk this game until the casino industry becomes fully cognizant of these new high-tech attacks on its "unbeatable" wheels. Once that happens, a simple countermeasure will be invoked that will stop the cheaters cold: Change the rules so that no bets are allowed after the ball has been released.

Summary

I'm sure I don't have to tell you that what Keith and Margo have accomplished is cheating, plain and simple. Even though it's a high-tech accomplishment, it's no different from stringing a slot machine, or shaving dice, or crimping cards. High-tech doesn't make it any less illegal.

Now you know why casinos spend millions of dollars each year on surveillance and security. They have to. Keith and Margo are just two. There are literally thousands of players just like them, maybe not as sophisticated, but every bit as ambitious. The goal: To win at any cost. Electronic gadgets are the new high-tech way to reach that goal.

It's interesting to read about such incredible endeavors. But it's not for me, and I trust it's not for you.

Play the games fairly, even though you know the games aren't fair. That's the deal you agree to when you walk in the door. You know the odds are against you. And for some, that only makes the challenge all the more exciting.

It does for me.

But in the case of roulette, heed my advice: Go easy on this game, and it will go easy on you.

Remember our No. 1 rule: If you can't afford to lose it, don't bet it.

CHAPTER 9

Slot Machines:
Rules Of The Game

You wouldn't believe how many slot players there are, roaming the aisles of casinos from California to Connecticut, who just can't understand why anyone would bother reading a chapter about how to play slots, much less why someone would actually write one.

Well, let me give you some reasons why slot players *do* need to read up on what they think is merely a matter of pulling a handle or pushing a few buttons and crossing two fingers. Here's what I see when I watch most slot players:

What's Wrong With These Pictures?

Scene 1: Here's a scenario that plays out so often, and is so significant a problem, that I want to give you two views to remember it by:

A player is working on a machine that pays a jackpot of 20 times the one-coin payoff *if* five coins are played. That's quite a bonus! How many coins is the player inserting? Sometimes one, sometimes two, maybe three, never five.

Another player is sitting at a bank of progressive machines with a common jackpot that grows as more coins are fed in by the players. But players must insert the maximum number of coins to win the giant jackpot. How many coins is this player feeding in? Sometimes one, sometimes two, maybe three, never five.

Evaluation: Please! Never build up a jackpot that you aren't trying to win! Some progressive machines might reach such an inflated jackpot total that the percentage advantage actually swings in your favor! At the very least, progressive jackpots will help mitigate the house advantage. Slot machines with realistic progressive jackpots are a favorite of knowledgeable players.

Playing the maximum number of coins is important for non-progressive machines, too. If there's a decent bonus for playing the maximum number of coins, you must do it! If the maximum number of coins—usually five coins—is too steep for you, drop down to a lesser-priced machine.

By not playing the maximum coin-in, as the casinos call it, you're adding to the percentages against you. That's right. The machine's overall hold (the casino's term for machine percentage) always takes into account the top jackpot. If you don't put yourself into position to at least have a chance at it, you're giving up an added five to ten percentage points. Readers with a mathematics background might want to learn more about this added hold percentage attributable to large jackpots. I explain it fully in the chapter on slot machines in my book *Casino Games*.

Always check out the jackpot payouts for maximum coin-in. Compare it to the payout for one coin-in. If it's a five-coin maximum, a linear payout progression would simply be five times the one-coin payout. If that were the case, there would be no percentage advantage to playing the maximum of five coins. But this is rarely the case. **Virtually all slot machines today offer a bonus payout for maximum coin-in. It's usually anywhere from ten to 20 times the one-coin payout. Learn how to evaluate this critical aspect of slot-machine design before you play.**

PAYTABLES	COINS PLAYED				
	1ST	2ND	3RD	4TH	5TH
Linear	250	500	750	1000	1250
	No percentage advantage in playing multiple coins				
5th Coin Bonus	250	500	750	1000	**4000**
	Significant advantage in playing maximum coins				

Some machines have more than one pay-line and reward you for maximum coin-in by adding additional pay-lines. These machines are simply called *multiple pay-line*. Still other machines simply increase the number of symbols for maximum coin-in. These machines are called *option-buy,* and are becoming the most popular. A typical option-buy machine might offer only cherries to win with one coin; bars are added for potential wins with two coins; 7s, the jackpot symbol, are activated with the third coin.

Single Pay-line
ALL PAYS ON CENTER LINE
(More coins increase payout; jackpot on last coin only)

Multiple Pay-line
1ST COIN ACTIVATES CENTER LINE
2ND COIN ACTIVATES TOP LINE
3RD COIN ACTIVATES BOTTOM LINE (JACKPOT)

Option Buy
1ST COIN ACTIVATES CHERRIES
2ND COIN ACTIVATES BARS
3RD COIN ACTIVATES SEVENS (JACKPOT SYMBOL)

It's not as easy to determine if playing all the lines on a multiple-line machine, or buying all the symbols on an option-buy machine is the smart thing to do from a percentage perspective. In fact, it's impossible for anyone to figure without inside knowledge of a particular machine. My sources at the manufacturing level tell me that players who only buy one line of, say, a five-line machine, or just one coin's worth of symbols on an option-buy machine, are probably giving up the better part of the game in terms of overall percentages. Those comments confirm my suspicions that playing maximum coins is the smart move on these types of machines, too. But there's another reason why you should play maximum coin-in on multiple-line and option-buy machines:

Let's say you only have the first two lines of a three-line machine activated. Or let's say you only bought cherries and bars on the option-buy machine, deciding against inserting that third coin to buy the big red 7s. Since you can only win the big jackpot on the last line of the multiple-line machine, or only win the big jackpot by lining up 7s on the option-buy machine, how do you suppose you're going to feel if you line up the 7s, or see the jackpot symbols click into place on that last line of the multiple-line machine?

That's right. I'm talking about the line that wasn't lit up because you were too cheap to put in another coin. The jackpot staring you in the face is worth ten thousand dollars!

That's TEN THOUSAND DOLLARS! One hundred pictures of Benjamin Franklin! But for the sake of a lousy quarter, you're out ten big ones.

Can you live with that? Can you just write that one off? I don't think so. That colossal screw-up will nag you for the rest of your life! I implore you: Do not risk the aggravation!

Heed this cardinal advice: Whether the machines you play are 2-coin, 3-coin, or 5-coin, whether you play progressive or non-progressive machines, whether the machines are single pay-line, multiple pay-line, or option-buy, you must play the maximum number of coins.

Some newer machines in casinos today require more than 5 coins to win the giant jackpot. Don't fall victim to this greedy marketing ploy. **Avoid machines that require more than 5 coins to win the jackpot.** Feeding in 10 or 20 coins at a time, or playing off 10 or 20 credits at a time is ludicrous. It flies in the face of what *Budget Gambling* is all about.

Scene 2: A young couple is fascinated by the casino's new video game that looks like a real dealer dealing real cards. It's incredible technology. And what does it cost to play this machine? Dollars. Are there frequent hits? No. Does this couple really want to play dollar machines? No. Can they afford it? No. So why are they playing it? Because the machine designers were right on the money in their evaluation of the new breed of slot player: Give the players a dose of virtual reality and they'll forget about percentages. The *real* reality. Like so many other younger players, they'll chalk it up as a cost of "entertainment."

Evaluation: This new variety of slot machine concerns me perhaps most of all. Newer slot machines have become more than just a gambling device; they have become a form of entertainment, no different from a pin-ball machine.

Let's not lose track of why you play. You're not looking for free games, you're looking for jackpots. And are you looking to be entertained? I hope not. I can think of much cheaper forms of entertainment.

Clearly, your goal must be to win. To win as much as you possible can. If you want entertainment, go to the movies. As soon as you start thinking of gambling as entertainment, you've fallen victim to the casino's ploy of blurring the distinction.

Incidentally, some of the newer machines are like three machines in one. The new video poker machines are a prime example. You're not playing one hand; you're playing three hands! At a dollar a pop, five coins in, three hands at a time, your cost of "entertainment" is $15 a game! *I've seen players with over five-hundred dollars in credits walk away from their machines just minutes later with nothing! Nothing to show for it! Nothing to cash in!*

Do you know how to quit when you're ahead? Most players don't. The new machines in casinos today are designed to encourage you to play. And play. AND PLAY! The casinos even have their own term for it. It's called "extended play." Don't fall for it. **You are playing to win! You are not playing to be entertained.**

If you're fortunate enough to win, make sure you leave with your winnings!

Scene 3: An older gentleman is playing video poker. He's found a machine that pays five coins for a flush and six coins for a full house. He doesn't know that a better machine is widely available in other casinos that pays *six* coins for a flush and *nine* coins for a full house.

Most players assume that the paytables are all the same. They aren't!

160

Evaluation: *Video poker is the only slot-machine game where you can actually determine a machine's percentage by noting the payouts on the different winning hands.* Although it's becoming more difficult today to actually rate machine percentages because of so many new paytables, you can at least determine whether or not one machine is better than another. All you have to do is look at the payouts. All machines display the payouts right on the screen!

POPULAR VIDEO POKER PAYTABLES

COINS PAID OUT									PERCENTAGE	
JKs	2PR	3K	ST	FL	FH	4K	SF	RF	W/JKs	W/O JKs
0	1	3	5	6	9	25	50	250	—	66-68%
1	2	3	4	5	6	25	50	250	92-94%	73-75%
1	2	3	4	5	8	25	50	250	93-95%	74-76%
1	2	3	4	6	9	25	50	250	96-98%	76-78%

Shown here are four of the more than 50 paytables available that you are likely to see in the casino. Note the importance of whether or not the machine pays on jacks-or-better: nearly 20 percent! This chart is based on the first coin inserted. Fifth coin/royal flush pays 4,000 coins.

The most widely used variable among the manufacturers today is the payout for a flush and a full house. Jot down the one-coin payouts the next time you play, and compare these payouts to other machines at other casinos you frequent. You might be surprised.

The new trend today in video poker is called "bonus features." There are at least a dozen different variations, the most common of which is called "Double Bonus Deluxe." But all of them have one thing in common: additional jackpots at the expense of smaller wins. In addition to the royal-flush jackpot, you might find a bonus jackpot for four aces, as an example. Or maybe a specifically suited straight flush pays a nice jackpot, too. There are so many new variations that it would be pointless to list them all. And I'm sure that more are coming. Who knows what lurks in the minds of these machine designers.

But again, one thing is a certainty: The lure of the bonus jackpots tends to obscure the loss of the smaller wins. A common example is the change in the paytable for two pair. Instead of a two-coin payoff, you'll "win" at even money, which isn't a win at all. The absence of wins for two pair more than makes up for the bonus jackpot.

My advice always has been to stick with the fundamental game. You can identify it by the payouts for the flush and the full house: 6 and 9 coins respectively. Casinos call these basic machines 6-9. There are 5-8 and 5-6 machines widely available. Obviously, look for the 6-9. And make sure you get a two-coin payoff for two pair. Jacks-or-better must return your bet. It's even-money but it sure beats losing the bet. You'll get a jacks-or-better pair over 20 percent of the time.

Remember, the tendency with video-poker machines today is for the casino to give you something new but take something away. It can't come as any surprise that what it takes away is worth more than what it gives you.

If you love to play slots but are completely unfamiliar with video poker, let me give you a crash course because this is THE game you should be playing.

The machines are based on a popular poker game called "five-card draw." When you insert five coins, or play off five credits, five cards will appear on the screen. The idea is to make the best poker hand possible by discarding as many cards as necessary and then "drawing" new cards in their place.

If it just so happens that you're not the "Maverick" of your hometown poker club, allow me to give you the "rank of hands" so that you'll know when to draw to that inside straight. Of course, there's no "hold 'em and fold 'em" stuff to learn because this is a machine you're playing against, not a table full of card-sharks, which is why the machine-version of the game has exploded in popularity. There's no rush. No bluffs. And you've got your own *Budget Gambling* game card to take with you to help you determine if, when, and how many cards to draw.

RANK OF POKER HANDS (in descending order)

HAND	DESCRIPTION
Royal Flush	Only the 10, jack, queen, king, and ace of the same suit.
Straight Flush	Any five cards in consecutive value, of the same suit, such as 2, 3, 4, 5, and 6 of diamonds.
Four-of-a-Kind	Any four cards of the same value (all four cards of the four different suits) such as the 8 of hearts, diamonds, spades, and clubs.
Full House	Five cards that include a pair and three-of-a-kind, such as a pair of kings and three 10s.
Flush	Any five cards of the same suit, such as 8, 10, jack, king, and ace of hearts.
Straight	Any five cards in consecutive value, not of the same suit, such as 4 of clubs, 5 of hearts, 6 and 7 of spades, and 8 of diamonds.
Three-of-a-Kind	Any three cards of the same value such as three queens.
Two Pair	Two pairs of equal-value cards such as two 3s and two 10s.
Jacks-or-Better	Any pair of jacks, queens, kings, or aces.

Scene 4: A new player is attracted to a carousel of machines with a multi-million-dollar jackpot. She doesn't know that these machines are almost always "sucker" machines, holding a much larger percentage than those with "down to earth" jackpots.

Evaluation: Let me tell you here and now that big multi-million-dollar jackpots are not worth the time and money to go after. Oh sure, there are many winners of these big jackpots who are happy they did, and more power to them, but come on... do you really think *you* have a chance? Well, you do. About 15 million to one! Your quarters, or dollars, will do you a lot more good in your pocket... right where they belong, as you walk right past these barkers of the casino's midway.

***Budget Gambling's* sub-title is "Bet little and win big!" But slot machines with super-sized jackpots are NOT the way to do it.** Let's find out why.

Even though casinos might promote a relatively low percentage on these machines, the percentage quoted must take the big jackpot into account. After all, the casino is figuring on paying someone... sometime! Well, take that big jackpot *out* of account, as you should, and all of a sudden you're bucking percentages on the order of 15 to 20 percent, maybe even more.

The casino knows it will have to lay a big check on some very lucky player. They don't know exactly when. No one does. But to be prepared for it, the casino removes about ten percent of all the coins the machines have won and tucks this money safely away in an escrow account. This ten percent is *in addition to* the regular hold (the quoted percentage) of perhaps eight to ten percent that the casino earns on these machines every day.

The escrow works as a hold against you, too. The money, after all, was *your* money. It's a big part of all the player's money that has been lost to these lying sidewinder machines. You didn't think the casino was going to pay the big winner out of its own pocket, did you? Nope. The losers pay the winners.

What it really boils down to is this: Literally tens of thousands of players pay one winner. And I bet you've never been thanked by a big winner before, have you? Neither have I. What's worse, those lucky million-dollar winners thought the casinos gave all that money to them out of the good graces of their own hearts.

Scene 5: A group of players are lured into a casino by a sign that says, "Our slots return over 98%!" When they get in, they find there are only a few machines identified as having this 98-percent return. And they are all being played! So, since they've gone this far, they decide to play other machines in the casino, not knowing—but they *should* know—that these other machines have much lower paybacks.

Evaluation: Don't let a casino bait and switch you!

After enduring a lot of bad publicity, Nevada casino operators in the early '90s stopped their practice of advertising low percentages that were not typical of all machines throughout their casinos. But that doesn't mean you can't get hoodwinked by some goofy, too-good-to-be-true promotion today. You can. They are still churning out gimmicks that sound good on the marquee, but smell like sardines when you get inside. Gimmicks have long been the lifeblood of casinos in highly competitive markets. For some reason, slot players seem to be the butt of most of them.

You'll still see promotional slogans such as: "Our slots are the loosest in town!" I have no idea what that means or how you could ever verify it.

Here's one that sounds good: "Play our can't-lose slots. A winner every time." Yeah. Each pull costs you three bucks and the "prizes" you get are carnival-type trinkets like key chains and cheap jewelry.

And my favorite: "Free-pull slot machines!" If you only knew what you have to go through to get a coupon so you can get a token so you can stand in a long line... well, now you do. But you can still wonder what the percentages are.

The whole idea behind these zany promotions is to get you inside.

Scene 6: A player's favorite bank of quarter machines have, all of a sudden, been changed to 50-cent machines. She wasn't prepared to play at this level, so she walks through the casino, look-ing for other quarter machines that she might like. But there are few to find. The last time she was in the casino, just a few months ago, there were plenty of quarter machines to play. Now she's stumped. She walked the maze, and she's in a daze.

Evaluation: It's a common ploy. *If you can't find the machines priced to fit your budget, leave at once!*

Casinos today are notorious for screwing around with their floor plans. Once you think you've got it figured it, the whole layout changes again. It's a clever way to mask the fact that a whole bunch of quarter machines—your favorites—have just morphed into 50-cent machines.

An Atlantic City casino operator told me all about it a few years ago. And he should know. He pioneered the concept of what he calls "cyclical pricing." At the time I talked to him, he was "converting" Atlantic City, having worked his way across the country, I guess, educating the gaming trade in all the major venues. Basically, the idea is to set up a huge promotion for the casino, and fill it up with quarter machines. Then leave it intact for a while as you naturally build up your customer base. As soon as your number of customers reaches a certain plateau, raise the prices to the next level—gradually though, over the course of, say, six months. The progression continues as some of those 50-cent machines grow into dollar machines over the next period.

The idea is to constantly build up the average machine price while trying to be somewhat subtle about it. Then, after the casino has maxed out its profit potential from the cycle, it starts all over again with another 25-cent promotion.

I've always said that the best marketeers in the country are casinos. They have to be. In hotly competitive markets such as Las Vegas and Atlantic City, all the casinos have to fight with are their promotions. Think about it. They have basically the same games—the same product. And they all have hotels with nice restaurants, big swimming pools, and rooms that all look alike. They need their promotions. The question is: Do we?

Here's a brief chart to help you find the coin denominations you're looking for. From a distance, you can look for the "candles" installed on the top of all slot machines. These candles are color-coded as to coin denomination. The candles light up to attract slot attendants when a machine malfunctions or when a jackpot has been hit requiring an attendant-payout. But we can use them, too, to help us quickly identify the coin values.

HOW TO TELL MACHINE COIN VALUES

CANDLE COLOR	COIN VALUE
YELLOW:	25 cents
ORANGE:	50 cents
BLUE:	$1
GREEN:	$25

Scene 7: A frustrated player is loading up a machine that is just like the one she plays at a different casino. But this one isn't paying. Yet she defies logic and continues to play... and lose.

Evaluation: Machines that look alike on the outside are not necessarily alike on the inside. Slot machines are ordered by the casinos with a specific percentage of hold. It's an arbitrary call. Believe me when I tell you that the percentages vary widely from one casino to another. You are wise to play only in competitive markets. But don't assume anything.

It's been said that casinos in non-competitive markets will survey casinos in highly competitive markets to see what design of machine is the most popular. Then, they'll order the same machine but with higher percentages.

Let me tell you a popular theory about machine percentages fostered years ago before the casino industry exploded in the '90s. Players believed that the best-paying machines were those located near the main entrance, or near restaurants and snack bars, or at the end of rows... wherever the most people would congregate.

That theory was soon blown out of the water when confidential casino floor plans were passed around showing that the percentages of machines varied very little from one part of the casino to another.

But today, with the competitiveness of the casino business at an all-time high, this theory is back in vogue. And this time there might be some truth to it. The new generation of casino operators might very well have taken a cue from this earlier myth. But take it for what it's worth. Don't take it to the bank!

The best test of all is to simply watch machines being played. Get a read on them yourself. See if they are really paying off. Let someone else do the testing for you! It can be a fun part of your gaming experience... and it won't cost you a penny!

I should also mention here that there is a general consistency in the distribution of percentages as they relate to machine pricing. A nickel machine, if you can find one, is generally regarded as having the highest percentages overall. A dime or quarter machine is next, followed by 50-cent machines and dollar machines. High-roller slots—those taking tokens of from $25 to $100—are regarded as having the lowest percentages. It makes sense. Few experts on the gaming scene will disagree with this notion.

COIN VALUE	AVERAGE SPREAD OF PERCENTAGES
5 cents	10–15%
25 cents	6–12%
50 cents	4–10%
$1	3–8%
$5	3–5%

Reel-type machines only. Actual percentages vary widely as to market and specific casinos. Generally speaking, the low side of the spread is found in most Nevada markets; the high side in Atlantic City casinos and on cruise ships; the middle and high side on riverboats and in Indian casinos; the low side and middle in Midwest and Gulfport markets.

Scene 8: A woman at a video-poker machine is playing off credits with such remarkable speed that each game lasts only a few seconds. It's clear to anyone watching that she only wants the royal and she's going after it with abandon. To spare you the trite cliché... with *costly* abandon.

Evaluation: Speed is no guarantor of success. Slow down and enjoy the moment. You can have just as much fun, if not more, at a relaxed pace. We've talked about it in each preceding chapter: You must learn how to cut down on the number of decisions. The more times you pull the handle, the further you go toward the long term. Remember that you can't win in the long term. So why rush into it? **Discipline yourself to control the speed of your game, whether at the slots or the tables, and take frequent breaks to stretch your stake.**

What seems to go along with speed in the casino is recklessness. Players who speed through the games are almost always hell-bent on a big win. There's nothing wrong with a big win, but there *is* something wrong if you throw common sense away to get it.

We've all seen video-poker players hit a royal; we stand around admiring the beauty of the 10, the jack, the queen, the king, and the ace, all sitting there proudly, all wearing the same suit. Even though it's on someone else's screen, we behold its beauty... its rarity.

The winning player is paid off handsomely by an attendant and told to play it off while the attendant watches. It's hard to play it off because it's hard to say goodbye to the royal family. They don't come out in public—together—very often.

What I'm leading up to is the truth behind the facade. There is such a strong drive to see the royals—almost an addiction, really—that the real question is, who pays for the front-row ticket? Does the casino pay you, or do you pay the casino? There are too many cases of players throwing away smaller wins—win after win—just for the opportunity of drawing, say, three to a royal. These players are easy to spot. You can always identify them by the way they play: Fast!

Go ahead and wonder. You have every right. Wonder how much it cost them to coax out the royals. *Winning, sometimes, only looks like winning.*

Scene 9: "That lady went ballistic," said the slot attendant, "when she saw that old man sit down at her machine and hit the big jackpot. I mean, it was the very next pull! On *her* machine! Can you believe it?!"

Evaluation: Most slot players think the same way. They just don't understand today's high-tech slot machines. The slot attendant doesn't, either.

If you read the opening chapter to *Budget Gambling,* you already know "what's wrong with this picture." That's right. The old man did not take the woman's jackpot. If the woman had stayed at her machine and played it one more time—instead of the man playing it—she would not have been as fortunate. That jackpot came as a result of the time that the man pulled the handle. The exact time... in milliseconds.

To put it another way, **the machine was not waiting for the next pull to deliver a jackpot. Don't confuse today's computer-controlled machines with yesterday's mechanical museum pieces.** And even if that were the case, there's a legitimate question as to whether or not the jackpot would still happen. But with today's machine, there's no question it *wouldn't* have. You see, a processor—just like the one in your computer—selects random numbers generated at lightning speed to determine what sequence of symbols will appear on the reels. That poor lady would have had to complete the action of pulling the handle at the exact same fraction of a second... within one millionth of a second... to rightfully claim "her" jackpot.

Indeed. The jackpot was his, fair and square. It wasn't a matter of who was sitting at the machine, or who pulled the handle. The only determining factor was *when* it was pulled. And for that, the gentleman was playing a different game... splitting hairs... and, like the woman, he probably didn't know about it, either. It's a little game that goes on *inside* the machine that controls the game *outside* the machine.

Scene 10: An older couple looks for two adjacent machines that they can play, with little regard for the machines themselves. They settle in, insert their slot-club cards, and play away. The losses mount, but they continue playing. They have no notions about finding a different pair of machines, even no notions about quitting.

Winning would be nice but their main goal is to get the free buffet tickets. They already have their two-night stay covered; now all they want to do is cover their dinner.

Evaluation: This is what I call, "playing for points," and it's exactly what the casino wants you to do.

A slot-club card serve two purposes for the casino:

First, it provides valuable accounting information for the casino's marketing department. Remember that application you filled out? Well, now the casino knows all about you. And they can track your play. They know what you play, when you play, and how you play. Having your vitals on record means the casino can market you (some casinos even sell their list of members to mailing-list companies who in turn sell it to who knows who). The casino can tantalize you with free offers in the mail, tournament announcements, and contests galore... whatever it takes to get you back to the machines. **Own a slot-club card and you've lost your anonymity—something that I will not part with when I visit a casino. I will not trade anonymity for annoyance.**

Second, slot-club cards tend to make you play in a manner inconsistent with winning. Although most casinos have tweaked their slot-club promotions, some still offer useless gifts such as T-shirts, baseball caps, and even beach towels. Whenever I see a guy wearing a baseball cap with the casino's logo emblazoned on it, I know that he must be very proud of it. It's probably the most expensive cap he's ever owned!

Members of slot clubs tend to forget their goal when they play. They look for higher-priced machines to get more points, or simply play longer—and faster—than they usually would. **You can be assured that the value of your rewards, whether in cash, comps, or prizes, rarely exceeds the losses you can run up as you let the casino's clever marketing control the way you play.**

It's what a gambling friend of mine calls playing "under the influence." I can't think of a better way to put it.

Some players even consider slot clubs as a status symbol. They proudly open their wallets and display nearly a dozen cards from casinos all over the country. Hey, we're not talking country clubs here... we're talking casinos, for gosh sakes. The cards are free for the asking. Any idiot can walk up and get one.

I find it interesting that several other authors writing on this subject take a totally different viewpoint. They encourage you to play with slot-club cards, telling you to try to get as many freebies from the casino as you can finagle. (I wonder if the casinos pay them a commission!)

But in the big picture, this advice is arguably wrong. **Most players are not disciplined enough to partake of the card's advantages without partaking of its disadvantages.**

Now, if it just so happens that you think you are so disciplined that you can play in the exact same manner you would *without* the card, not letting the perk-potential influence you in any way, then go ahead and get your card. But heed one more example:

I just got back from Vegas where I met a friend of mine at the casino where he was staying. I invited him to come with me to the casino where I was staying, telling him that the video-poker machines at my place had the best payouts I've ever seen. But he wanted to play at *his* place. I couldn't understand why. The machines at his place had lousy payouts. "But John," he said, "I've got over a thousand points over here. Two thousand points will pay for my room. I need to play here."

"No," I said. "Playing these sub-average machines is what will pay for your room. For what you're giving up, the casino should give you a suite!"

Scene 11: A grandmotherly lady is concerned that she hasn't won in several trips to her favorite northern Nevada casino, in spite of all her efforts to play so conservatively. She has just changed from quarter machines to nickel machines, but now she's losing at a higher rate than before!

On this most recent trip, she finds a nickel video-poker machine at a different casino and is overjoyed. But as she studies the machine's paytables, she can't believe what she sees: To have a chance at the royal-flush jackpot, she must play 20 coins!

Twenty coins! Twenty profiles of Thomas Jefferson is one classic portrait of George Washington! **This isn't a nickel machine! It's a dollar machine in disguise!**

Would she dare play less than 20 coins and risk losing the bonus payout if she lines up the royal? She decides that she can only play five coins because she can't afford a dollar a pull. The whole idea of playing nickel machines was to go easy, and now it looks like the casino has made it impossible for her to even have a chance at the bonus jackpot.

She has fallen victim to a clever ploy.

She has played into the casino's greedy hand.

Evaluation: Here's a scene that presents a dual paradox to all slot players. It's a true story that this kind lady reported to me at about the time I was finishing this chapter. It struck me that two of the vary things I've already covered were happening to this poor woman in her futile attempt to enjoy *Budget Gambling*. She wanted to play nickel machines but the percentages were too steep. She wanted to play nickel machines but the 20-coin max was absurd.

Seasoned players have long suspected that nickel machines hold a higher percentage for the house. And we've already proved that. These same players also believe that it is wise to start out with nickel machines, and progress upward to quarter machines if winnings prevail. And they're basically right again. It's a tenet of *Budget Gambling*— start small, and build up winnings! But 20 coins?! That isn't small!

So how do we deal with this conflict? We want to play nickel machines, if we can find them, because our budget tells us to. But why should we pay such a price? Why should we be penalized for conservative betting strategies?

Why? Because the casino has it all figured out. *Casino executives reason that if they are going to settle for smaller bets, they want to make a bigger return.* So, the nickel machines hold the most, the dollar machines—and especially the high-roller machines—hold the least. At least that's the way it's supposed to play out. (To refresh your memory, look again at the chart of machine percentages vs. coin value a few pages back.)

And just to make it all the tougher for a nickel player to win, casinos have now raised the ante:

Instead of 3- and 5-coin machines, there are 10-coin, 20-coin, and even 40-coin nickel machines designed to catch you off-guard. Nickels add up, too. Don't be fooled by the casino's clever tactic.

In spite of the casino's greedy attitude about making money, I still have to support the notion of starting out with nickel machines. I'm talking 3- and 5-coin machines, of course. Not the high multiple-coin machines that are an insult to sensible slot players. Until the nickel machines eventually phase out, or the percentages mount even higher, I'll stick with my recommendation to start out with five-cent slots as a safe, budget-minded starting point in your climb up the denomination ladder.

For those players who make the same comparison between quarter machines and dollar machines, the same relationship does hold. Generally, quarter machines hold more than dollar machines. If nickels just aren't your speed, or you can't find 'em, then start your climb with quarters.

However, **never be suckered into a high multiple-coin machine that requires more than five coins to win a bonus jackpot.**

Scene 12: I'm right behind a young couple walking up the deck to a riverboat casino, and we're both headed to the same place: the coin attendant's station, to break larger bills into more digestible sizes for those hungry video-poker machines. I notice they both have two twenties and they want four tens. I'm impressed already. They plan to play in ten-dollar sessions. Smart. Very smart. I hope they take long breaks in between. But they do have a problem. And I'll bet they don't even realize it.

Evaluation: On this particular trip to north-western Indiana's riverboats, the problem these players are going to have is a problem that I'm going to have to deal with, too. My wife, Kathy, and I make this little jaunt about once a month. That's right. I do have to keep in shape, you know.

But for this trip, anyhow, Kathy and I are going to have the same problem the other couple will have. It's just that I didn't know it at the time. Kathy figured that I was going to finance her. I usually do. But I thought she had stopped by the bank that morning and loaded up with our usual two hundred apiece.

No, she didn't. We each had to settle for whatever we could scrounge out of our pockets. **We do not do the ATM scene. We do not finance our gaming with credit cards.**

Fortunately for us, the winds were howling that day so the boat didn't go out, which meant the doors stayed open. That was good, because we both were a bit resigned to the fact that we might very well be walking through those doors again sooner than we had planned. Maybe not the most positive way to look at it, but I believe in being realistic before being positive. Clearly, our bankroll of about seventy-five bucks apiece—we split the booty—was going to be a little tough to stretch over the dice tables and video poker. Particularly, the dice tables!

Bankrolls are relative. What's reasonable for me might be too little for you. And too much for someone else. But that's not the point. Our greatly compromised stake put us in a position that would affect the way we usually play. There was no question it was having a negative effect on both of us.

A gambling trip with too little bankroll is not a matter of conservation, it's a matter of plainly not having enough ammo to get the job done. What if the dice tables and the poker machines were cold right out of the chute? Well, I can tell you. They were. And you can't ride it out with nickel this and nickel that. You can take a break, but when you return to the games what if the dice and the poker machines were cold again? Well, I can tell you. They were. And you find yourself trying to save bullets.

By the third session, we were unprepared for our improving opportunities because we did not have the confidence that only a solid bankroll can give you. You play overly cautiously. You can't bluff your aggression when it's time to strike if you have only a few shots left. A short stake usually results in only one thing: A short session. And it did.

As we walked off the boat, we came upon the young couple who had even a shorter stake than we did. They were wiped out, too. We arrived at the same time; we left at the same time. We all had simply made it too easy for the casino to beat us.

Here's what I told the other couple when it became clear to me that they were thinking about getting more money and going back on the boat:

"No. The trip's over for us. It should be over for you, too. We didn't come prepared with enough ammo."

"We didn't, either," they said. "We can't afford much more than a couple twenties between us, but we know that we should bring more."

"You should," I said, "but understand why. You don't want to bring more money just to lose it. If you think that way, that's exactly what will happen. Let's say you bring one hundred dollars each, but each of you set a loss limit of fifty dollars. You'd be surprised how much better you'll feel, knowing that if you lose the fifty, you still have fifty left in your pocket. That fifty left in your pocket is not to spend, but to walk out with. There's no worse confidence-wrecker than gambling with the fear that you might have to walk out flat-busted.

"And another thing. If you look over your past performance at the machines, or at the tables, you might be surprised to know that sometimes that hot hand or that hot machine you're looking for doesn't surface right away. It takes time. It takes staying power. It takes bankroll. Just be sure you don't use it as an excuse to lose more!"

On our way home, we stopped at a favorite restaurant of ours along the Lake Michigan shore that serves up a great bowl of chili. When it came time to pay, I gave the waitress my Visa card.

"We don't take credit cards, sir."

"Jeez, you don't?! Well, uh, what are the damages?"

"Nine dollars and sixty-four cents."

"Oh, well, let's see."

Kathy dug all the way to the bottom of her purse. An area that even Jacques Cousteau hasn't explored. There was enough stuff in there for a guy to set up a small retail shop. And there was enough change to cover the bill—if the restaurant didn't mind all the pennies—and we found some more change in the car, enough to tip the waitress, although I think she *did* mind all the pennies.

At least we didn't have to do dishes.

CHAPTER 10

Slot Machines:
Budget Gambling
Strategies

Before I show you the right strategies, let's talk about the wrong ones... strategies that *don't* work. And I could fill this book with them. All kinds of crazy superstitions and misconceptions abound, passed along from player to player, even spanning generations from mother to daughter. That's right, slot systems are a family affair. You hear these wacky claims so often, from so many different players, that you start believing them, too. Slot players take them very seriously... almost religiously. The gospel according to Fred.

Well, they can take them to the casino, but they can't take them to the bank!

Here are my favorites:

1. Hot coins/cold coins. You've probably heard this one. It's been around since slot machines became "electrified" in the '60s. And just to show you how screwy this "strategy" is, it has two opposing versions: One theory says that you only play machines that pay out in warm coins, because that means the machine has been holding on to the coins for a good while and is now ready to pay out.

The other theory, exactly the opposite, says that you should only play machines that pay out in cold coins because the machine has apparently paid out all the warm coins, which is evidence of a "pay cycle."

Oh, brother! Coins get warm because of the heat generated by the electronic components in the machine... you know... transformers and power supplies and rectifiers and capacitors, and stuff like that. These things don't have a clue about what's going on up there where the reels are, the real important stuff, right? Plus, the coins can get hot from the light bulbs that light up the feature glass on the lower front section of the machine, which just so happens to be situated about where the coin hopper is.

I talked to an old friend of mine at a slot-machine manufacturing company to find out exactly how long it takes for coins to warm up once they've dropped into the hopper. He got a chuckle out of my question, and asked me if I was using the "hot coin" or "cold coin" method. I said, "No, it's not for me, it's... uh... for a friend of mine."

"Yeah, right," he said. "Tell your 'friend' that all the coins are going to be warm to the touch in about two hours. It takes that long," he said, "because the lighted panels use cooler, more efficient bulbs." Obviously, coins today don't get as hot as with older-model machines. He also said that most of the old hopper designs, many still in use today, drop coins from the bottom but receive coins from the top. So, virtually all of the coins will at least be a little warm... assuming a full hopper.

The only logic that might be construed from the theory of playing only cold-coin machines is—and this is a heck of a big stretch—that a machine dumping cold coins hasn't had a chance to fill up the hopper because it's been too busy paying out!

Hmmm. Before this starts to actually make sense, let's get on to the next one...

2. Slow pay/fast pay. Slot players know that some machines pay out fast, and others spit out coins as if they just don't want to part with them. Similar to the cold-coin theory, the myth here is that a slow-paying machine is trying to find coins to drop from a nearly exhausted hopper.

Again, the idea of an empty or nearly empty hopper is a good sign... supposedly. But many machines today siphon off coins before the hopper fills up. Newer machine designs have smaller hoppers that spill into an "overflow" hopper. Once the main hopper starts to fill up, additional coins played into the machine merely bypass this smaller hopper and go directly to the larger hopper. Some casinos do call it an overflow hopper; others call it a portable hopper. I call it a bucket.

At any rate, if the hoppers are spilled before they fill up, and if the hoppers aren't as big as you thought, what does that say for any system based on the number of coins stored in the hopper? Not much.

You should also know that the "counter," a mechanism that actually dispenses the coins, is made by several different companies for the slot machine manufacturers, and... wouldn't you know it... some go lickety-split, while others are slow as molasses. Maybe the manufacturers get a better deal on the slow ones. Or maybe the casinos actually specify the slow ones. Who knows? Who cares?

3. Mechanical/video. There remains a die-hard following of slot players who will not, under any circumstances, trust a video slot machine. They like the good ol' mechanical machines, and that's all they'll play. They believe that any machines with a screen can be rigged to beat you.

Well, of course they can! And they are! I'm not sure that "rigged" is the right word, but believe me, they are "rigged" to pay back something less than what is paid in.

Younger slot players take the opposite view of the old-timers. They think that the older-looking mechanical machines are easier to rig—a screwdriver adjustment, for example—to increase the percentages against you.

Well, no they aren't. But that doesn't mean that they have better percentages, or that they are more "trustworthy" than a newer video-type machine.

There are two factors that enter into play here. One, **whether your favorite slot machine has a**

**screen or actual moving reels is incidental to the
way percentages are determined at the factory.
And that's where they are set. Not in the casino.
And certainly not with a screwdriver. Because
today, changing percentages means changing a
circuit board.**

That's right. And that's the other factor you
should know. All slot machines, whether they look
like they are mechanical or not, are now controlled
by a computer. You probably thought the video
machines were computer-controlled, but I bet you
didn't think the mechanical-looking machines were,
too. Well, they are.

**When you see the reels click into place, just
as the really old machines used to do, there is
no spring or other metal parts that randomly
perform this task. It's the computer chip inside
that tells the reels where to stop.** The instant you
pull the handle or push a button, the chip selects a
random number that corresponds to a reel-stop combination.

The slot machine manufacturers call these machines "micro-processor-controlled mechanical
machines"... thank you very much... but I call them
"misleading." With today's demands from slot players for bigger and bigger jackpots, the concept of a
computer-controlled mechanical-looking machine
was not too hard to imagine. If players wanted
these mechanical look-alikes, and they wanted the
big jackpots, too, the only way to make it happen
was by "rigging" them up to a computer chip.
Otherwise, there simply were not enough stops on
the reel, not even enough reels, to provide all the

reel combinations (literally millions) to be able to offer the bigger jackpots.

If you've picked up some tips from slot players of yesteryear when machines were honest-to-gosh mechanical, I should warn you about the advice you might have heard. Forget pulling the handle a certain way. Forget drilling holes in the side of the machine to insert wires. Forget looking for worn metal parts that might produce a bias. Forget "stringing" the machine (tying a string to the coin so you can yank it back out).

Oh, and forget magnets, too. That "strategy" has been around since slot machines were played for a slug of chewing tobacco The only thing that a magnet will do today is shut down the machine. And instantly alert Security.

Optimum Strategy

As unbelievable as it might seem, there actually is a strategy that can, over the long term, show a profit for slot players. Notice I said, "can," not "will." It's another one of those strategies, like blackjack card-counting, that looks darn good on paper, works great in practice, but comes up a bit short sometimes in the real world of noisy casinos where the cards just don't fall exactly the way they're supposed to... like they do "on paper."

Still, it's worth a mention, because I know there are legions of slot players out there who would just love to be privy to such information. So listen up.

Since video-poker machines are the only one-armed bandits that flaunt their percentages right in your face, you might be able to get the jump on one of these guys and beat him to the draw. Yep. This strategy only works at the video-poker machine. So bone up on the game. Get a copy of Dwight Crevelt's *Video Poker Mania* and learn the right moves. Go ahead! Develop a skill! A skill that will set you apart from all the other "ordinary" players who would rather just stick a nickel in and close their eyes.

In the preceding chapter, we talked briefly about the difference between a 5-6, 5-8, and a 6-9 machine. Learn how to recognize these important variations. And, if you remember, learn how to avoid the casino's new-fangled machines that *appear to be* better. Stick with the basic 6-9 machine where you know exactly what you're up against.

On a 6-9 machine, you're playing against a house percentage that is remarkably low... on the order of two percent, maybe a fraction more. I'm assuming, of course, that you are playing the optimum way, making few, if any, mistakes in your draw decisions. But a little ol' two percent advantage against you, although pretty good, isn't going to win the marbles. You need to shift the percentage to *your* side. And you can do that on progressive machines.

Although most video-poker progressives use 5-8 machines, you can still get the edge if the royal-flush jackpot exceeds a certain level.

Let's assume you're playing a 5-8 quarter machine, so a 4,000-coin jackpot correlates to a $1,000 win. The percentage against you on the 5-8 is higher than the 6-9 because of the short-pays for the flush and full house. Let's go with the generally accepted figure of five percent. But let's say we've found a 5-8 quarter progressive machine and the meter above the carousel reads $1,500. Such a significant increase in your jackpot potential eats away some of that percentage against you.

The only way you can beat the machine with a fair modicum of consistency, however, is by landing the royal. If you don't get the royal, chances are the machine will take a chunk of your money no differently from what a straight machine would do... over the long term, of course. That's why you must make your draw decisions without error. And you must play from a bankroll that can survive the ups and downs of such a valiant try.

Although there are differing opinions on how large the jackpot has to be to swing the edge in your favor on a bank of 5-8 progressive machines, I like to use the 120 percent rider as a basis for determining whether or not I want to tackle it. A 120 percent rider means the jackpot should be $2,200 on a 5-8 quarter progressive carousel. That puts us slightly ahead of the game, on paper, and we'll just have to see if we have the stamina to see it through.

The downside to this strategy is obvious. Just because the jackpot is so high, and just because you can play the hands perfectly, and even if you have an unlimited bankroll, there certainly cannot be a guarantee that you'll hit the royal. If for no other reason, some other player might hit it before *you* do! Hey, that's the chance you take. Worse yet, the likelihood is slim that you'll even find an open machine to play when the progressive jackpot is so high.

Years ago, casinos that offered progressive video poker carousels with 5-8 machines were bombarded with "professional teams" that took over all the machines when the progressive meter topped two grand. They would march in at 4 a.m. when the machines were usually sitting idle, and take them over... literally holding the machines captive. The casino's regular customers complained, and many casinos reacted by establishing stringent rules about team play. Still, it goes on, and some players do make out... like a bandit.

Budget Gambling Strategies

I really can't give you a charted strategy for playing slot machines as I've done for you with craps, blackjack, roulette... and horse racing in the next chapter. You can't vary your bets; in fact, you shouldn't, so that wipes out any idea that we could play a progression.

The million-dollar jackpots that only require three quarters for maximum coin-in would seem a likely choice for a proposition strategy, but, as you've learned in the preceding chapter, these machines with the eye-popping jackpots must be avoided.

Some machines today allow you to parlay your winning wager with a "Double" feature that gives you the option of doubling a win (a double-or-nothing bet). If you lose it, you lose your winnings. In most cases, the house picks up a nifty eight percent on this wager. That's an *extra* eight percent! Don't do it!

So what I want to do is list some of the things that you *should* do. For all slot players, for all machines, for all the times you play. If you follow this list, you'll be a better play for it. I'll promise you that. But that's all I can promise. If the next time you leave the casino, you leave with a $50 loss instead of a $150 loss, we should both be pleased... not real happy... but pleased. And if you should leave with a $500 win instead of $100 win, we will both be pleased... and happy!

The Do-Only Strategy

1. **Make sure your bankroll fits your game.** Don't be under-financed. But don't be over-financed, either. Either of the extremes can be a problem. My advice is to find your comfort level and stick with that same bankroll amount for all of your gambling trips. If your trips vary in length, assign a certain stake per day. The key here is continuity. Drastic variations in your bankroll can have a negative effect in the way you play.

2. **Do not rush to play.** Upon arrival at the casino, be prepared with something else to do first. Temper your anxiety. It might be something as simple as having breakfast or lunch, or meeting friends over coffee. Maybe you've had a long flight or a long drive. It's absolutely essential that you change gears, relax, and get in

the right frame of mind before you challenge the machines.

3. **Observe before you play.** There's so much that can be gained by simply watching. Particularly if you're thinking about a certain bank of machines. Watch the other players. Although you can't be assured that all the machines sport the same percentages, you might learn from watching that more walking is in order. At the very least, judicious observing helps you by minimizing exposure.

4. **Always play the maximum number of coins.** I've given you all the reasons why in the preceding chapter. I can only hope I have convinced you. Remember, some machines today take more than the typical 3-coin or 5-coin maximum. I've seen some machines that take up to 100 coins! Obviously, our play-the-max rule only applies to 3-coin and 5-coin machines. Watch out for the new arcade-style 10-coin machines or the new "triple" machines that are really three machines in one. Players tell me these machines are hard to resist. My advice is to steer away from "gimmick" machines of this sort and stick with the standard 3-coin and 5-coin paytables.

5. **Begin with relatively small bets.** Regardless of what machine price you choose, determine your range of play and start at the bottom. Most players have a range of 25 cents, 50 cents, and one dollar. If your range is a little lower, start with a 5-cent machine if you are fortunate

enough to be playing in a casino that still offers them. If you can afford to start higher, you should, because you've already learned from the preceding chapter that nickel machines have the highest hold percentage of all denominations. Still, if that's all you can go, that's where you start.

6. **Move up to higher machine prices as you continue to win.** At least you can utilize the advantages of a progression this way. If you've won a considerable amount on a quarter machine, move up to a 50-cent machine. If a dollar machine has filled up several buckets for you, why not try a $5-token machine in the high-roller pit. But use common sense. If the move up immediately sours, what are you going to do? You either drop back to the bottom price of your range, or quit. It's not complicated. Quitting isn't complicated.

7. **Play in sessions with a specific loss limit per session.** We'll borrow this one from the Four Color Strategy. When you reach your loss limit, the session is over. Take a break. Take a long break. Setting loss limits makes all the sense in the world. Setting win limits makes no sense at all. If you're winning, keep playing! Play as long as you win! Winning streaks come along so rarely that you must really take advantage when it happens. *Remember, always set a limit on your losses, but let your winnings run!*

8. **Avoid speeding.** Here's another item we've covered earlier. I'm sure you now know how

damaging a fast game-speed can be. So slow down. Enjoy yourself. I've always believed that most players really don't want to play fast but they feel pressured to win or pressured to "get even." Everyone has internal regulators. If your biological clock simply runs too fast, let it wind down before you play. Otherwise, you might find that gambling poses a destructive conflict for you. And don't forget that a relaxed pace helps reduce long-term exposure. In any negative-expectation game, the faster (or longer) you play, the more likely you will lose.

9. **Never play when you are tired or upset.** This is particularly true if you're playing a skill game such as video poker. But no matter which game you play, being tired or upset can lead to serious errors of discipline. Attitudes change when you're not sharp and alert. Why risk a serious financial setback? It will just give you something else to be upset about.

10. **If you can't afford to lose it, don't bet it.** Yes, you've heard this expression before. Although it's become a worn-out cliché, I would like to restore it to its full faith and meaning. Listen to it every time you put your bankroll together, every time you reach into your wallet, and every time you make a wager. So, you're going to the casino with $500. Can you afford to lose it? And be honest with yourself. If a $500 loss will sting you, don't risk it. Gambling should be on the very bottom of the list of things you want to do with your money.

CHAPTER 11

Horse Racing: Rules Of The Game

In the second chapter, I mentioned that all the games that would follow, chapter by chapter, were in the order of their worth for *Budget Gambling*. I started the run of game chapters with craps because that game fits the concept of *Budget Gambling* to a T. Under the right circumstances, I believe it is the best place in the casino to turn that proverbial toothpick into a lumberyard. Indeed, the concept of betting little and winning big is embodied in this streaky game.

Still, horse racing should have started the run of game chapters. It should have been first in line, and no doubt would have been if I had been writing this book 20 years ago. But the horse-racing scene has changed so dramatically over recent years... changes that have had great negative impact on the rewards of handicapping.

Some would say that horse racing is largely a dying institution. Many of the minor tracks around the country have closed up, sold to developers who saw more value in the land than in the track itself. And larger tracks are feeling the same pressure. Even at the major tracks, bettors complain about small fields of horses. Sure, some races may go off with only five or six horses running, but they do go off. That beats betting on bulldozers clearing the way for a housing development.

Bettors don't like small fields of horses because that usually means small prices. It's a hand-me-down problem. There are fewer horses in the races today because there are fewer horses foaled! Breeders have seen the signs and simply are not producing as they used to, or they've become, well, housing developers.

With fewer horses, there are fewer jockeys. And they have to make a living, too. So, they move to other tracks while younger jockeys move in and take their place, if there is a place to take.

It all boils down to attendance. Which is dwindling. Sadly, there's a one-word answer as to why: Attrition. You see fewer young couples at the tracks today. Most of the patrons are senior citizens, brought up on horse racing during its glory years of the '60s and '70s.

Until the managers of the industry stop blaming other things for the decline, and look hard at their own product, the drop in the gate and the resulting drop in the purse-money will surely continue. There is no marketing savvy, no casino-quality promotions. Nothing is being done to attract the young players who want more excitement for their gambling dollars.

Actually, there is a move underway to attract these players, but it doesn't bode well for the sport. The racing industry, in its divine wisdom, has come up with a one-word solution: Slot machines! OK, two words. Sure, slots will bring in tons of players! Tons of *slot* players! Slot players who couldn't care less about who's racing in the eighth. For those tracks that have already tried this weird cross-marketing of two competitive "sports," the results are in:

Says a slot player: "I like the slots, but I don't like it when the races go off. It bothers my concentration." Says a track owner: "I don't want a racetrack with slot machines. I want slot machines with a racetrack."

It's a commentary I would prefer to spare you, but if I'm going to talk to you about betting horses, you need to know what's going on. Now you've got the picture.

The Two "Pluses" Of Horse Racing

Compared to the casino scene, horse racing is a slow game: two minutes of exciting racing followed—and preceded by—30 minutes of waiting. A period when the old-timers are studying the next race. I personally don't believe the youth of our great country are too much into studying, do you? Can you imagine going to the casino to play blackjack, burying your head in a blackjack book for half an hour before you plunk down each bet?

But horse racing is obviously different from blackjack, and this "negative" really isn't one at all. Remember, one of the key elements of *Budget Gambling* is a game-imposed, or self-imposed, reduction in the number of decisions you wager on. Horse racing certainly fills the bill, and that's one of the reasons it's included in this book. A track-junky I know calls it "stake preservation." And he's right. You can have an exciting afternoon of thoroughbred racing (or a fun night at the harness track) and make maybe a dozen bets at the most.

Which leads us to the other "plus" of horse racing: low risk, high rewards. With only a few dollars at risk, you can take your best shots with the potential for huge payoffs! As you'll soon learn, there are short-odds and long-odds bets that you can make, and we're going to concentrate on the relatively longer odds of what the track calls "exotic" wagering. But there's nothing exotic about it at all. In fact, these popular bets you are about to learn are the real lure of the track. It's just that we're going to make these bets a bit differently than most handicappers do, in the hope of beating the odds and walking away with fistfuls of money!

Study Hall

There's another alleged downside of horse racing... a negative in the minds of many of the few beginners who come along... and it's a negative that I can't turn into a positive. It's the "studying" part of the game. You can't just pick horses on a

whim; you need to study what is called a racing
form (or a "program" at the harness tracks), which
contains the "past performances" of the horses.

I'm not a proponent of spending untold hours
behind a pair of reading glasses with a racing form
clutched tightly in one's grip. It works for some,
but it doesn't seem to work for the younger players. Not many of them, anyhow.

Over 500 horse-racing books have been published over the years, but few of them are actually
about horse racing. The purpose of these books is
to show you—in 384 pages—how to read a racing
form. That's right. Inside these books are all the
tips you need to find something in "the form" that
has—incredibly—escaped all the other handicappers.

For each day of racing at every thoroughbred
track around the country, the racing form provides
a record of each horse's recent races. An information sheet, if you will, of detail after detail, so you
can produce a "system" for picking winners.

Let's see, bet the horse that's still a maiden
(hasn't won its first race), that's not a shipper
(shipped in from a different track), that races well
on grass (horses race on both turf and dirt), that
gained in the last quarter (didn't quit in the stretch),
that has dropped in class (racing for a smaller
purse), that drew an inside post (close to the rail),
that finished in-the-money in its last outing (2nd or
3rd, in this case), not coming off a turn-out (has
recently raced), that is racing a longer distance (a
route vs. a sprint), that carries the same jockey
(the short guy in the clown-suit with the whip).

If you're like me, and not that interested in putting this much effort into handicapping, but you still think you would like to go to the races, you're in luck. I'm going to show you a way in the next chapter to bet horses *without* studying! Without even *buying* a racing form. You won't *need* a racing form! The other handicappers will make your decisions for you. But not just the regulars. You'll learn how to detect what the *smart* handicappers are doing. Then *you* can do it, too! There's nothing like having someone else do your homework for you! The youth movement will love this!

The Basics

I'm going to assume that you know little, if anything, about the mechanics of horse racing, so the remainder of this chapter will be devoted to the basics of wagering. It's not complicated, so I'm going to give you a crash course. This will be like cramming for an exam. A lot of information in a few paragraphs. Pencils ready. Here goes:

There are usually nine or ten races on the program at a thoroughbred track. Harness tracks might have as many as 13 races.

Most thoroughbred races are scheduled every 30 minutes. Harness races rarely have more than 20 minutes between them.

Thoroughbred races are different lengths, from a mile and three-eighths to six furlongs. **A furlong** is one-eighth of a mile, so a six-furlong race is three-quarters of a mile. The longer races are called **routes**. Shorter races are called **sprints**. Virtually all harness races today are one mile in length.

Harness-racing horses are called "standard-breds," and are either **pacers** or **trotters**. The difference is in the gait: A pacer "paces" by moving a front leg and opposite rear leg simultaneously. A trotter "trots" by moving both the front and rear leg of one side simultaneously. If a standardbred **breaks** into a gallop, the horse must be "pulled up" and placed by the driver at the end of the field.

Most races are either an **allowance race** or a **claiming race.** An allowance race (called a "conditioned race" at the harness tracks) states certain conditions for which a horse can be eligible, such as purse money earned, number of races won, and age or sex of the horse. For example, a race might be conditioned as, "Fillies and mares, non-winners of 4 races lifetime." In the case of thoroughbreds, an allowance race may also include additional weights to carry relative to purse earnings. A claiming race is for horses that may be bought (claimed) by any licensed racehorse owner for a specific claiming price. There are also **stakes** races in which the owners of the horses pay a fee to be entered.

You can bet a horse to **win** (finish first), **place** (finish first or second), or **show** (finish first, second, or third). You can also bet an **exacta** by picking the two horses that will finish first and second, in order. Some harness tracks use the term **perfecta** instead of exacta. A **quinella** is just like an exacta except the horses do not have to finish in exact order. A **trifecta** is just like the exacta except you must pick the *three* horses that will finish first, second, and third, in order. To win the **daily double,** you must pick the winners of the first and second race. Some tracks now offer a second daily double later in the program.

The minimum bet you can make is two dollars. There is no maximum limit because all bets are **parimutuel,** meaning that the winning bets are all paid from the total of all bets made for that race, called a **pool**. The track does not bank the bets as a casino does; instead, it takes a certain percentage of money from each pool, called a **takeout,** to pay purses and overhead and make a profit.

The more money that is bet on a particular horse, the lower the **odds** (the payoff expressed as odds to one, such as 3 to 1. The odds continually change as bets are made, and are displayed on a **Totalizator,** a large, lighted, scoreboard-like panel usually installed in front of the grandstand. Other smaller displays are installed throughout the grandstand and clubhouse.

The amount of money you win, therefore, depends on how many other players also won. If you were among many winners because the **favorite** (the horse with the lowest odds) won, you will win only a token amount. If, however, you picked a winning **long-shot,** a horse with higher odds because few other players made bets on this same horse, your winning ticket will be worth much more.

After each race, the Totalizator will display the **prices,** the values of winning tickets. The prices are all based on a two-dollar wager and include the return of this theoretical two-dollar bet. So, to convert the prices to odds, simply subtract two and divide by two.

Totalizator displays these prices:

	WIN	PLACE	SHOW
1ST	8.00	4.20	2.80
2ND		3.00	2.40
3RD			2.20

$8.00 TO WIN converted to odds to 1:
Simply subtract $2 and divide by 2:

Win $8
     −2
     6   Divided by 2 equals 3 (3 to 1 odds)

You will win three times the amount of your wager, and your wager will be returned to you. If you wagered $5, you will win $15 and collect $20. If you simply add one to the odds—in this case, 4—that number will tell you how much you will collect (4 times your wager).

This simple formula saves a lot of grief trying to determine exactly how much you won with, say, a $15 ticket (3 x $15 = $45 *in winnings*).

Many handicappers do it the "old-fashioned" way and divide the amount of the ticket by $2 and then multiply by the price, $8 in our example ($7.50 x 8 = $60 *to collect*).

But my easier way has another advantage of showing you exactly what the odds were at the **post** (at the time the race went off). And it follows the casino standard of quoting payoffs in "odds to one."

All tracks provide a program that gives you basic information about each race that day, including a rundown of the horses entered, their **post position** (the gate from which the horse leaves—

the 1st post, also called the 1-hole, is closest to the rail), the name of the jockey, and, of key importance, the **morning line.** A track handicapper assigns odds to the field of horses in each race, which becomes the morning line, also known as the "opening line," or "program odds." Based on these early odds, the track handicapper will also list the horses he or she believes will finish 1st, 2nd, and 3rd. These horses are referred to as the **program picks,** and usually carry considerable influence among bettors.

At the harness track, the program is more detailed than at the thoroughbred track, and usually provides all the information you would normally find in the thoroughbred track's racing form. The horses' post-position number is clearly displayed on the **saddle cloth** of the horse so that you can identify a particular horse during the race. A standardbred, however, also uses a **head number** because sometimes the harness equipment obscures the number on the "saddle" cloth.

Another important distinction between thoroughbreds and standardbreds is the way the race goes off. Thoroughbreds leave from a portable **starting gate** that is fixed in a particular location on the track depending on the length of the race. The race begins when the doors to the gates all open in a quick, simultaneous action. But at the harness track, the starting gate is not stationary; it's attached to a car equipped to hold this different kind of gate that resembles a trackwide fence. The car moves slowly at first, building up speed, while the horses gradually move up to the gate. When it is determined that all the horses are "up and on the gate," the gate opens from a center hinge and swings away from the horses. The race is off as the car speeds away.

It's interesting to note than one of the track **stewards,** an official of the racing commissioner's office of that state, not an employee of the track, is seated in the car and makes the decision when to start the race. The steward continues to monitor the race from his position in the car. Most races today utilize three stewards who are responsible for the fairness of the race and for determining the official outcome. They also cite infractions by fining or suspending trainers, jockeys, and drivers, and, in some cases, by **setting down** a horse, which means moving a horse down in the official order of finish. Sometimes, a horse may be disqualified.

When you see the term **official** appear on the Totalizator, you know that the stewards have reviewed the race, concluded it was fair, and assigned the order of finish. Until the official sign is lit, the race is unofficial, even if a listing of finish appears on the board. *Always hold on to your tickets until the official sign is lit.*

When you go to a track, you will find it's a little different from going to a casino. For one, the track will charge you for parking. General parking is cheap but usually is a cab ride from the track. Preferred parking, which is closer, is expensive. Next, you'll have to buy the program, which is not cheap, either. And, if you want a racing form, that's a few more bucks, too. If you want to sit in the **grandstand,** it's open seating, but get there early

for a good spot. If you would prefer a nicer sur-
rounding, try the **clubhouse,** but you'll pay extra
for this, too. How do I compare the grandstand to
the clubhouse? You'll eat hot dogs in the grandstand; you'll dine on filet mignon at your white-
linen table in the clubhouse.

The procedure for actually making your bets is
no big deal. But there's a perk to betting in the
clubhouse, as you might expect. There are more
ticket windows so you should not have to stand in
long lines. Since making late bets is a crucial aspect of the way we're going to bet horses in the
next chapter, you'll see that a clubhouse table is
probably well worth the extra investment. Scribble
on your program exactly what you want to bet and
take the program with you to the window. Have
your money ready.

There is a correct procedure for telling the ticket
writer what you want. If you follow it, the whole
thing will go smoother and faster. First, tell the
writer the amount you want to bet, then the kind of
bet, followed by the horse number. For example,
if you like the 3-horse to win and you want to bet
five bucks, say: **Five dollars to win on the 3.** The
writers don't want to know the name of the horse,
just the number. And they push the buttons to record
and print out your ticket exactly in the order I've
listed. That's why it's the most efficient way to do
it.

Incidentally, it's always assumed that the bet
you're making is for the next race. If you're betting a later race, then begin your instruction with,
"In the seventh race...."

Return to your table, take another bite of that juicy steak, sit back, and relax. Oh, and take good care of your ticket. Anyone can cash it if you lose it.

Neat Things To know

- If you live in the Midwest, chances are an exacta is called a perfecta. It's the same bet, just a different name.

- Another way to box two horses for an exacta is called a **quinella.** To win the bet, you must select the two horses that will finish 1st and 2nd, in *either* order. A $2 quinella and a $1 two-horse exacta box cost the same. But be careful... a winning quinella ticket might be worth more, or less, than half of the exacta price.

- When the track announcer says, "Hold all tickets," it usually means one of three things has happened: (1) The finish was too close to call so a **photo** needs to be developed and studied to determine the official order of finish. (2) One of the stewards in charge of the race suspects that an infraction occurred during the race so an **inquiry** is called. A review of the video tape of the race, sometimes from different camera positions, will be made. (3) One of the jockeys or drivers suspects an infraction occurred during the race so an **objection** is called, resulting in a review of the race.

- Inquiries and objections can lead to a horse being **set back** which means to be placed in a lower finish position than the unofficial finish.

Depending on the severity of the infraction, a horse may also be **disqualified.**

- Once the official sign has been lit, or the track announcer states that the race is official, the prices that are posted on the tote board stand. Sometimes, however, subsequent action by the stewards, or the state's racing commissioner, can result in a redistribution of purse money.

- Sometimes two or more horses are coupled together as a single betting interest, called an **entry.** If the horses are owned by the same owner or trained by the same trainer, the entry is called a **mutual entry.** Horses in an entry have the same post number (such as 2 and 2A) but obviously do not leave from the same post.

- A term that seems to confuse new bettors is **mutual field.** The term simply means a grouping of horses, other than an entry, that is considered one betting interest. A mutual field is made whenever the number of horses in a race exceeds the capacity of the Totalizator. Generally, the highest number on the tote board is assigned to all the horses with that number and higher.

- There are only two exceptions to the standard rule that payment is only made to bettors for the finish of the top three horses. In one case, a **dead heat** for show (3rd) will result in four horses finishing "in the money." A dead heat means a finish for any of the top three positions resulted in a tie, because the photo was unable to discern a difference in finish. In the other case, some tracks offer a **superfecta** wager that requires you to pick the top four horses in order.

- At the harness track, there might be a **recall** just before the race has started. A recall means the race will not go and will be restarted. Some of the reasons for a recall include: a horse that will not take to the gate, a horse that interferes with another horse, a horse that falls, or a horse that displays broken equipment. If a recall is charged to a particular horse, it must not cause a second recall or it will be disqualified. A recall is never made solely because of a breaking horse.

- The average cost today to attend a racetrack, including parking, seating, minimal food & beverage service, programs, and other forms, is nearly $20! And you still haven't made your first bet! But don't give up yet. Hopefully, the special *Budget Gambling* strategies in the next chapter will help you recoup your costs and send you to the winner's circle!

CHAPTER 12

Horse Racing: *Budget Gambling* Strategies

If we were to bet horses the way most handicappers do: by studying the racing forms and programs, hanging around the track, getting to know the trainers and jockeys, etc., we would not be doing what *Budget Gambling* is all about. By now, I'm sure you've picked up on what this unique concept is: low risk, high rewards—fun, easy, and profitable. Spend a few bucks, have some fun. And give yourself a chance for a big win!

Studying the forms... and I mean *really* studying... is not easy. Most newcomers would also say it is not fun. So that's not going to be a part of our strategy.

Hanging around the track... and I mean *really* hanging... is fine if you're (a) retired, (b) laid off, (c) a rich kid, or (d) a bum. But I'm assuming you're like me and actually have a job that occupies most of your time and is definitely required if you want to go out and buy groceries. So let's forget the idea of bumming around with the horses. Let's look at more sensible ways of making money at the track that better fit today's "do it now" lifestyle.

In the preceding chapter, I whetted your appetite with a subtle hint as to how *Budget Gambling* would apply to horse racing. I said that we'll let other handicappers do our handicapping for us.

Incidentally, the term **handicap,** in the context of horse racing, simply means "to pick." A handicapper is someone who picks horses to win, place, show, fill up a trifecta, or whatever. If you're betting horses, you're handicapping. If you're giving out advice on which horses to bet, you're handicapping.

There are two key reasons why we can rely on someone else's picking. "Rely" might not be the best choice of words. We really can't rely on anything. Handicapping at the race track is gambling, pure and simple. Let's just say we're going to "go with the flow" of certain handicappers who are much better than we are.

The Track Handicapper

The handicapper we first want to pay attention to is called "the trackman." It may not be the politically correct term, but that's what these people have been referred to in racing programs since day one. We'll use the term **track handicapper**. It's the responsibility of the track handicapper to set a "morning line" by assigning odds to each horse in a given race. At some tracks, the morning line may be referred to as "probable odds." These odds are clearly shown on the program, representing the likelihood of a particular horse winning. As a result of the assignment of these odds, three horses are picked as the program favorites. Obviously, the program favorites are the horses with the best odds.

Most programs will identify these horses at the bottom of each racing page with the heading: Trackman's Selections. A few tracks around the country do not spell out the three top picks at all, simply leaving it up to the bettors to figure it out themselves.

I want to make sure you'll be able to accurately determine the top picks just in case the track doesn't do it for you. Odds lower than 5 to 1 can sometimes confuse inexperienced bettors. It's important that you can distinguish among the rank of odds from lowest to highest. So, here's a chart of the typical odds you'll find at the racetrack, starting with the lowest odds (best chance of winning):

1-5	6-5	5-2
2-5	7-5	3
1-2	3-2	7-2
3-5	8-5	4
4-5	9-5	9-2
1	2	5

Odds greater than 5 to 1 are easy as pie. The odds will always be "to one," such as 6 to 1, 7 to 1,

8 to 1, and so on. As you look down your program, you'll quickly be able to tell the long-shots from the favorites, and be able to rank them as the track handicapper has done.

Of course, the program lists the horses in their order of post position, not in their order of odds. That's why you need to be able to do this simple chore. As I said, it's the lower odds that are tougher to rank, so always take along the horse-racing game card that came with *Budget Gambling*. The game card displays the Rank Of Odds to assist you. There's certainly no need to memorize it.

If we're going to rely on the morning line to help us cash winning tickets, it would be nice to know exactly how accurate the line is. In other words, just exactly how good is the track handicapper?

Well, at many tracks around the country, the track handicapper is really the "secretary of racing," which means we're relying on the person whose main job is to "write" the races by listing all the conditions for eligibility. The racing secretary then puts the **race card** together. The race card is the program of races for a particular day. It might include allowance races, claiming races, or stakes races. It's up to the racing secretary to put as many horses into a race as possible, and make the card the most exciting for the bettors.

In addition, the racing secretary is also in charge of "the draw," the actual process of assigning post positions to the horses. The secretary of racing is like a "program director" of a radio station. Instead of deciding which songs will be played, he or she decides which horses will race. So, as you might imagine, this person knows the horses, the trainers, the jockeys, and the track itself about as well as anyone. A certain reliance on the track handicapper's selections just makes good sense.

Racetracks conduct ongoing reviews of the track handicapper's performance because it is important that the picks are reasonably reliable. Setting realistic odds is important to the track just as it to the bettors in the stands.

Generally, a good track handicapper will pick the winning horse in one out of three races. With nine races on a card, the track handicapper will usually pick three winners. If the payoff for a "win" ticket would always be higher than 2 to 1, we could all quit our jobs and just hang around the racetrack. But most favorites go off at odds of 2 to 1 or less. In fact, a winning horse goes off as the "odds-on favorite" (at less than 1 to 1 odds) nearly 20 percent of the time. It's not too exciting to cash a two-dollar ticket and win a measly dollar. In fact, it's not worth the risk, either. Picking just the winning horse is not the way to make big money at the racetrack, and that's not the way we're going to do it, anyhow. But at least now you know just how good the track handicapper is. Pretty darn good.

Of course, the track handicapper doesn't just pick the winning horse. Technically, the job means picking *all* the horses, since odds must be assigned to each horse in a race. And here's where the real interesting stuff comes in. Now pay attention.

My own studies have shown that a track handicapper has an unusual tendency to select the winning horse as the 2nd- or 3rd-place pick. **In research-ing several of the major tracks, I've noted that the winning horse was picked 2nd or 3rd an uncanny 44 percent of the time!** Now that doesn't mean it's going to happen every time you go to the track. The track handicapper has good days and off days like everyone else. I remember one par-ticular card at a harness track in Chicago where the winners were correctly picked in every single race! And there were twelve races that day! Now that's uncanny! But if the track handicapper can pick all the winners, he can also *miss* all the win-ners. And that certainly does happen.

When I first began compiling research several years ago, I studied past performances just as other handicappers at the track did, except I was looking at the track handicapper's performance while other bettors were busy studying the horses! The results of my work from that era would be seriously skewed today for several reasons.

For one, there are smaller fields of horses today, which would certainly increase the likelihood of better handicapping. But I've also found that the track handicappers of yesteryear were just plain better than those today.

Another factor that needs to be plugged in for today's track handicappers is the changing field of horses. The game of racing has become more tran-sient today. Jockeys move around more from track to track, as do trainers and the horses in their barns. The old days of a "circuit" of horses, jockeys, and trainers moving from track to track as a meet closes and another one opens, is becoming passé. Clearly, there are factors that make it easier for the track handicapper today, but there are also factors that make it tougher.

Much of my research for this chapter has been "filtered" to reflect today's entire racing picture as best I can. For example, the bulk of my older information came from the days when I handicapped harness horses almost exclusively. In those races, the circuit was intact and the field of horses was usually eight or nine. Bettors could expect solid performance from the track handicapper, and they usually got it.

For this discussion, let's go with the track handicapper's capability of picking three winners out of nine races as a reasonable average to expect. Let's also assume that the track handicapper can find the winner within the 2nd or 3rd spots four races out of nine. So, out of nine races, the winner will come from the top three picks about seven races out of nine. An overall average over many years of research puts this number at 6.4 races out of nine, but let's go with 7 since races today are rarely filled as they were in the past. Remember this statistic because we are going to use it often in putting together our bets later on in this chapter.

Professional Handicappers

The other handicappers we want to pay attention to are in the grandstand or the clubhouse just as you and I, but with one big difference: They *do* study the forms, they *do* hang around the track, they *do* know as much, or more, than the track handicapper, and they wager big bucks to prove it. **Because "professionals" make such large wagers, we can usually pick them out of the crowd. How? By watching for significant changes in the odds as the wagers are recorded on the tote board.**

Another telltale sign is the timing of their wagers. These "pro" bettors—and that includes bettors who might have inside information—almost always make their bets late. Why? Because they don't want to tip their hand. They know that many bettors are looking for these large swings in the odds as a signal as to which horse to bet. Unlike the stock market, a hot tip at the track brings *down* the price of a horse. The more people betting it, the lower the price.

Sometimes it's difficult to spot these sudden increases in wagering, especially at major tracks with literally thousands of bettors contributing to the tote board. Since the bets we're looking for are made late, these particular bets become a smaller percentage of the pool as the betting continues. The odds may not change as dramatically the later it gets because the percentage increase becomes less significant, so you will have to keep a keen eye on the late odds as they change. Generally, the tote board updates the odds about every five minutes.

Here's what we have so far: We're going to look for late money, late *big* money, as a tipoff to what the pros think. But we'll use this information judiciously, coupled with the information provided us by the track handicapper, in making our own selections.

There's a term I purposely didn't define for you in the preceding chapter on the basics of horse racing, even though it certainly belongs under "basics." I didn't tell you about it then because I wanted to save it for this chapter. And now's a good time to highlight it. The term is **shut out.** It's what happens when you don't get to the window in time to make your bet. Ticket machines lock up at the start of a race. Obviously, a racetrack needs protection against accepting bets after a race has started. A bell rings at the ticket windows when the race goes off. If you're still standing in line when you hear the bell, you're out of luck.

It's an important fact to deal with, since the bets we're going to make will most often be made late. So learn which ticket writers are the most efficient. Learn to identify bettors who take too much time. Above all, make your bets from the clubhouse, where there's usually a higher ratio of ticket writers to bettors than in the grandstand.

Optimum Betting

Bettors who support themselves financially by handicapping horses have one goal in mind: to find the winning horse. They are not looking for an **overlay,** a racing term that means a better price than the horse's past performance would warrant.

I hear it all the time. A bettor says, "I don't like such-and-such a horse because the price isn't high enough." Even though the horse was carefully picked out to win, the bettor is going to continue looking because the odds were too low. It's what I call, "looking for a horse to beat the winner." The pros don't think this way at all. They find the winner, and then they bet the winner regardless of the price.

There's something else the pros don't do. They never bet a horse to place or show. Always to win. To win! No daily doubles, no perfectas, no trifectas. To win; that's their name of the game, and it should be ours, too, if we were to take the long and bumpy route to becoming a professional handicapper.

How often do you suppose they find the winning horse? You might be surprised to know that they cash only one or two tickets a day. But they may only bet two or three races! That's right. Most of the time, the pro handicapper is just watching. Picking up valuable information for future races. As a racing pro told me many years ago, "If I'm not absolutely convinced a horse is going to win, I pass."

Trifecta

As is so often the case, the optimum way of gambling is not the most exciting. The optimum way to bet horses, as you've just learned, is for a rare kind of individual. I doubt if it's you; it's certainly not me. And it certainly does not fit the concept of *Budget Gambling*. Rarely, for example, does the professional have a shot at a high multiple-odds payoff. The wins are modest but sweet. After all, the winnings are used to pay the bills. That same pro handicapper I quoted earlier is deserving of another quote: "For me, the wins are not so much exciting as they are satisfying."

For us, we *want* excitement. We want to enjoy the sheer anxiety of chasing a dream ticket. And that dream ticket, more times than not, is a trifecta treat.

To refresh your memory, a winning trifecta bet means you correctly picked the top three horses in order. If we were to go to the window and say, "Two-dollar trifecta, 3-8-5," the race has to finish exactly 3-8-5. The 3-horse has to win, the 8-horse has to place, and the 5-horse has to show. This bet is called a **straight ticket.** Any other order and your ticket is on the floor.

Trifecta Box

There's a better way to bet three horses in a trifecta. It's called a **trifecta box.** Let's say we "box" the 3-5-8 instead of just playing the straight ticket. Now, the horses can fill the top three spots in *any* order. Boxing three horses means you are really making six different bets. There are six different ways that three horses can finish. The ticket would cost you $12 (6 wagers at $2 each), but you can also make this bet for $1 a wager, so the ticket will only cost you $6. If you win, you'll get half of the trifecta price.

The downside of a three-horse trifecta box is that you still have to pick the three horses that will finish in the top three spots. How much easier it would be if we could pick four horses, or even five, and box them. Well, we can do that, too, but it's gosh-awful expensive. A $1 trifecta box of five horses will set you back $60, and you'll only get half the pot! Hardly fits the bill for *Budget Gam-*

bling, does it? No. That's not our solution. A trifecta box is not the way we're going to make our wagers. But since it's a common wager at the track, I want you to learn about it.

Incidentally, how would you like to make a bet that can't miss? How would you like a guaranteed lock to win the trifecta? Well, you can, by simply boxing *all* the horses in the race! Let's say there are eight horses racing. If you box all eight, the bet will cost you $336 for a $1 ticket ($672 for a $2 ticket). If the favorite wins, and there are no long-shots in the money (the top three spots), the trifecta might pay anywhere from $75 to $150 depending on how many other bettors also won the trifecta. It's even possible that the trifecta price would be a lowly $50 or so. If that were the case, you would have spent $336 for a $1 trifecta box that pays $25.

Of course, the race might have knocked out the favorites, allowing a long-shot to come in on top. Now that $336 ticket might look pretty good! I've seen trifecta prices as high as several thousand dollars. But is this the risk you want to take? No. Of course not. The trifecta box, no matter how many horses we plug in, is not the way to the roses.

The Trifecta Wheel

This bet confuses most new bettors, but it doesn't have to. The **trifecta wheel** is designed for handicappers who like to pick a certain number of horses to finish on top, a certain number to finish 2nd, and a certain number to finish 3rd. That's it.

No big deal. But sometimes it's a little tough to figure out the cost of the ticket.

The trifecta wheel has a lot of advantages that we want to use. A typical trifecta wheel ticket has one horse picked to win (or it can be in either of the other two slots), and five other horses picked for the other two spots. A $1 ticket costs $20. A bit more reasonable but still too steep for *Budget Gambling*.

Another downside of this particular bet is that a certain horse you pick has to win. If that horse doesn't win, you lose. And the other two spots must be filled up by two of the remaining five horses. This still isn't what we want, but we're getting there.

The bet I like and use most often is called a **trifecta partial wheel.** Here's the basis for the bet:

We're going to pick four horses, total. Two of the horses can either win, place, or show. A third horse can either place or show, and a fourth horse can only show. That's it. We have four horses to work with. And, get this... our cost for a $1 ticket is only $8. Here's how it looks on paper:

WIN   1-2
PLACE   1-2-3
SHOW   1-2-3-4

To confirm that there are eight ways to win:

1	1	1	1	2	2	2	2
2	2	3	3	1	1	3	3
3	4	2	4	3	4	1	4

Here's the way you should think of this bet:
If the 4-horse is in the money, it must show.
If the 3-horse is in the money, it can't win.

224

So now we know the means to picking horses, and the ticket we want to write. All that's left is how to do the picking. After all, we can't always bet the 1-2-3-4, as in our example. We need different numbers to plug in!

Here's how we do it:

The Fine Art Of Picking Horses

On your program, mark the track handicapper's selections with a yellow highlighter by drawing through the horse's name. Now those three horses will be quickly discernible. Next, find all the horses with morning-line odds of 15 to 1 or higher and draw two diagonal lines through the listing from corner to corner with ink pen. The large "X" you'll create will be easily noted. These horses will have been eliminated from consideration.

Next, wait until nearly half of the betting period has elapsed. Typically, this is 20 to 30 minutes, so you'll be waiting no more than 10 minutes. At that time, write down the new odds from the tote board for all the horses in consideration. Most programs allow you room to do this directly beside the morning-line odds on the program. Note those horses (other than the yellow-lined picks) where the odds have been lowered. The best way of noting the horses with lowered odds is with a green highlighter. Draw a line with the highlighter directly above or below the horse's name. The length of the line will be determined as follows: the lower the drop in odds and the longer into the betting period, the longer the line.

As the race nears, the excitement mounts because time is now beginning to put pressure on you. You'll want to check the odds as late as you can before you put your bet together. To do this, you must be already in line if the lines are long, or at least standing near the ticket windows in case long lines begin to form. There are television monitors near the windows that display the same information found on the infield's tote board.

If the odds on a horse you've marked with a green line continue to drop, simply extend the green line accordingly. If the odds on a green-line horse begin to rise, do nothing. It's not unusual for a horse's odds to go down and then rise as the betting eventually rights itself. It's even possible that a horse you marked with a long green line will go to the post at its opening odds. You did your job; you caught the drop in odds; hopefully, your work will pay off.

Now we're ready to fill in the wheel. The two horses you will want on top are (1) the horse with the longest green line (if more than one horse has the same longest lines, choose the horse with the highest odds as of that moment), and (2) the horse with a yellow line with the highest odds as of that moment. These two horses will also be listed in the place and show positions.

The third horse to add to the place and show positions will have the next longest green line. Again, if there is more than one horse with the same length line, choose the horse with the highest odds among them.

The fourth horse to add to the show position will be chosen among the remaining two yellow-lined horses and any green-lined horses that are left. Simply pick the horse with the highest odds. It's possible that you'll be choosing among relatively high odds for this position, and that's fine. It's also likely that you'll have two yellow-lined horses in your wheel, which generally means the price will be relatively low if you hit it. Personally, I'm very comfortable having two yellow-lined horses in my wheel, and find that I sometimes bias my selection process for the 4th pick by not counting any remaining green-lined horses if the lines are really short. I'll let you tweak this aspect of the strategy yourself.

Now you know why it's important that you do not draw the green lines until about halfway through the betting period. If you begin marking the horses too soon, too many might be marked, which would tend to eliminate the two remaining yellow-lined horses from consideration for your show position. Most often, only one, two, or three horses will be green-lined.

When you get to the ticket window to make this bet, here's how you say it: "One-dollar tri, part wheel, 1-2, over the 1-2-3, over the 1-2-3-4." The ticket writer at the window will think you're an experienced handicapper and really know what you're doing. Actually, the ticket writer will find out if you "really know what you're doing" when the time comes to cash the ticket!

The odds of winning the trifecta with a part-wheel bet as I've listed here are hard to pinpoint, but they are probably not as good as you would like to believe. And that doesn't just go for you, it goes for anyone, regardless of the horse selection process used. Tri's are tough. Don't expect to win two or three every night. That's not going to happen. But, over time, I hope the high multiple-odds payouts make up for some dry spells. In *Budget Gambling* terms, this is proposition betting at its best.

You should also know that there are some situations where you won't be able to make the trifecta wager. For example, it's possible there will not be enough green-lined horses to fill up your wheel. You need at least two. If you can't fill it up, you'll have to pass on the bet. Which reminds me... don't make up your own rules just so you can make the wager. Not a good idea.

One of the reasons you might not be able to mark enough horses with green lines is because the favorites are getting all the money, in which case, the odds on many of the other horses will be rising instead of dropping. Don't hesitate to pass up a race.

In fact, I never bet a trifecta if the favorite is going off at less than even-money. The reason I won't bet is because I would most likely not have that favorite in my wheel. And I don't like going against a horse that looks that good on the tote board. But even if I did have the favorite in my wheel, and the ticket won, the price would probably be so small that it's hardly worth my $8 to go after it.

That's why my selection process always calls for the highest-odds horse available. If you find that betting the highest-odds horses is not working out for you, convert to betting the lowest-odds horses. You should win more often, but the prices will undoubtedly be smaller. I recommend that you add these two clarifications to your strategy.

Another reason you might have to pass on the trifecta is because the track is not offering the bet on that particular race. At the harness tracks, trifectas are offered on nearly all races, but not so at many thoroughbred tracks. Don't ask me why.

For those of you who do not have the patience for bets that win so infrequently, let me suggest an exacta wheel, which is far easier because you only have to pick two horses, not three. But, in line with the reduced odds, you should expect smaller prices.

The Exacta Wheel

We can do the exacta wheel just like the trifecta wheel, but we eliminate a level of selection. Here's how we go after the exacta, looking for the two horses that will finish 1st and 2nd, in either order.

We're going to pick three horses, total. Two of the horses can either win or place. A third horse can only place. That's it. We have three horses to work with. And, this is even better... our cost for a $1 ticket is only $4. Our ticket is simply a "one-two, over the one-two-three." Here's how our exacta wheel looks on paper:

```
WIN        1-2
PLACE      1-2-3
```

To confirm that there are four ways to win:

```
1    1    2    2
2    3    1    3
```

Here's the way you should think of this bet:
The 1-horse and 2-horse can either win or place.
The 3-horse can place, but it can't win.

Selecting the three horses for the exacta wheel is just like what we did for the trifecta. Mark the favorites with yellow lines. Cross out the long-shots. Wait ten minutes. Get out your green highlighter.

The two horses you will want on top are (1) the horse with the longest green line and (2) the yellow-lined horse sporting the highest odds as of that moment. These two horses will also be listed in the place position.

The third horse to add to the place position will be chosen among the remaining two yellow-lined horses and any green-lined horses that are left. Simply pick the horse with the highest odds.

Natural Progression

Horse racing lends itself to two progressive betting habits that I particularly like. First, you can start with a $1 exacta wheel and "progress" to a $2 wheel if you win. Second, you can start with an exacta wheel and "progress" to a trifecta wheel if you win.

Since one of the hallmarks of *Budget Gambling* is minimum risk, your starting point each time you visit the track should be a $1 exacta wheel.

Remember that a $1 wheel earns half the payoff. The prices on the tote board are always for a two-dollar ticket. And you should also know that an exacta is more than twice as easy (if *easy* is the right word) as a trifecta.

Starting with a $1 exacta wheel is the smart way to go.

Down The Stretch

As you get more accustomed to handicapping, you might actually want to do at least some studying to help you decide if you think the changing odds are correct. If you do get to the point where you want to review past performances, let me make clear exactly what you're looking for: **You are not looking for the horse that *should* win today. You are looking for the horse that *will* win today.** And there's a huge difference.

It's no different from the bane of sports bettors: watching a team lose that should have won; a team far superior in talent but one that inexplicably falls short on the scoreboard. A college basketball team, for example, might have a lackluster regular season, but come to terms with its potential for winning in the NCAA tournament. The smart handicapper will know that this team comes of age in the tournament. The makings were there: good coaching, teamwork, free-throw shooting, strong defense, and so on, but the team was rarely inspired during the regular season.

231

Believe it or not, horses are really no different. Sometimes they feel like racing hard and sometimes they don't. Like humans, they need motivation... a desire to win.

A good handicapper can look deep into a horse's racing performance in the hope of finding a clue that will lend predictability to today's race. Are all the conditions here that will spark that desire to win?

If I were to elaborate on all the points that can help you read the racing form, I might as well write the 535th book on horse racing, but that's not the intent of this chapter. I make mention of this simply so you can see that picking horses by studying past performances is a frustrating, grueling process. Only a few handicappers I know have the stamina and the analytical mind to make it work for them.

For the rest of us, *Budget Gambling* answers a lot of the concerns of new players. Take your game card with you to help you make your exacta and trifecta wheel bets. It's easy and it's fun!

I hope you decide to give horse racing a try. If you are fortunate enough to live near a major track, that's all the better. If you live in Southern California, for example, you can visit my favorite cathedrals of horse racing: Santa Anita and Del Mar. Other states are noted for horse racing, too: Florida, New York, Maryland, Ohio, Illinois, Kentucky, Arkansas, Louisiana, and Texas, for example, have great tracks steeped in rich tradition.

Keep the tradition alive.
Enjoy the sport of kings!

Other Great Gambling Titles
From Gollehon Books

Video Poker Mania (Crevelt)

Slot Machine Mania (Crevelt)

Casino Games (Gollehon)

Casino Games II (Gollehon)

Casino Gambling Behind The Tables (Alcamo)

Las Vegas Behind The Tables (Vinson)

Las Vegas Behind The Tables, Part 2 (Vinson)

Conquering Casino Craps (Gollehon)

The Book Casino Managers Fear The Most (Karlins)

A Gambler's Little Instruction Book (Gollehon)

Beat The Track (Kulleck)

Casino Comics (Lewis)

Deadly Deception (Engelhard)

A Gambler's Bedside Reader (Gollehon)